The
PARENT'S
GUIDE
to
BUSINESS
TRAVEL

A CAPITAL IDEAS BOOK,
practical books that offer expert advice

OTHER TITLES INCLUDE

How to Avoid the Mommy Trap:
A Roadmap for Sharing Parenting and Making It Work
Julie Shields

A Grandmother's Guide to Extended Babysitting: Practical Advice,
Inspiration and Space for Important Information
Ruth Meyer Brown

The Golden Rules of Parenting: For Children and Parents of All Ages
Rita Boothby

Mistakes Men Make That Women Hate: 101 Image Tips for Men
Kenneth Karpinski

Use Your Fingers, Use Your Toes: Quick and Easy
Step-by-Step Solutions to Your Everyday Math Problems
Beth Norcross

Father's Milk: Nourishment and Wisdom for the First-Time Father
André Stein with Peter Samu

The Man Who Would Be Dad – Hogan Hilling

The RAT (Real World Aptitude Test): Preparing Yourself for Leaving Home
Homer E. Meyer, Jr.

The 10 Biggest Legal Mistakes Women Can Avoid: How to Protect Yourself,
Your Children and Your Assets
Marilyn Barrett

Graduate! Everything You Need to Succeed After College – Kristin M. Gustafson

Honey, I've Shrunk the Bills: Save $5,000 to $10,000 Every Year – Jack Weber

Connecting to Creativity: Ten Keys to Unlocking Your Creative Potential
Elizabeth Bergmann and Elizabeth Colton

A Grammar Book for You and I . . . Oops, Me!
All the Grammar You Need to Succeed in Life
C. Edward Good

The Kitchen Answer Book: Answers to All of Your Kitchen and Cooking Questions
Hank Rubin

Your New Dog: An Expert Answers Your Every Question
Susan McCullough

The Dogs Who Grew Me: A Tribute to the Six Dogs
Who Taught Me What Really Matters in Life
Ann Pregosin

Dog About Town: How to Choose and Raise an Urban Dog – Pat Farley

ALSO BY CHARLIE HUDSON

Orchids in the Snow (Perrico Publishing, 1998, Novel)
Shades of Murder (Briarwood Publications, 2002, Novel)

The PARENT'S GUIDE *to* BUSINESS TRAVEL

Practical Advice and Wisdom for When You Have to Be Away

CHARLIE HUDSON

A Capital Ideas Book

CAPITAL
BOOKS, INC.
Sterling, Virginia

Capital Books, Inc.
P.O. Box 605
Herndon, Virginia 20172-0605

Library of Congress Cataloging-in-Publication Data

Hudson, Charlie.
  The parent's guide to business travel : practical advice and wisdom for when you have to be away / Charlie Hudson.—1st ed.
      p. cm.—(A Capital ideas book)
   Includes bibliographical references.
   ISBN 1-931868-11-5 (alk.paper)
     1. Parenting. 2. Parent and child. 3. Parents—Travel.
   4. Business travel. 5. Work and family. I. Title. II. Series.

   HQ755.8 .H83 2003
   649'.1—dc21

                                                    2002073759

Printed in the United States of America on acid-free paper that meets the American National Standards Institute Z39-48 Standard.

First Edition

10 9 8 7 6 5 4 3 2 1

Contents

PREFACE   ix

ACKNOWLEDGMENTS   xv

PART ONE—WHAT, HOW, AND OTHER THOUGHTS

CHAPTER 1

Introduction   3

The Realities of Separation   3

A Word About Separation Anxiety   5

A Military Flavor   6

How the Book is Structured: Parts One and Two   7

CHAPTER 2

How Long *Is* a Week?: Infant to Pre-Schooler (Up to Age Five)   10

Infant to Toddler (Age Two)   10

Ages Three to Five   14

Saying Good-bye   18

How About Those Presents When You Come Home?   18

CHAPTER 3

You Really Should See the Pandas: The Older Child   21

The Elementary Years (Ages Six–Ten)   21

Ah, Those Preteens (Ages Eleven–Twelve)   24

You Missed Trash Pickup Day?   26

Speaking of Coming Home . . .   27

A Note for Single Parents   28

Taking The Family Along   29

CHAPTER 4

A Different Approach for Teens 34

Adolescence First (Ages Thirteen to Fourteen) 35

The Core Teenage Years (Ages Fifteen
to Eighteen) 37

Home Alone—If and When 38

Remember Though, They're Not Adults Yet 40

CHAPTER 5

Hey Mom, My Arm Is in a Cast! 43

Sooner or Later 43

Thinking Ahead Won't Make It Happen 45

CHAPTER 6

Should I Be Traveling Anyway?—
The Debate Continues 48

Opinions and Studies Abound 48

Balance Doesn't Always Mean Equal 49

Warning Signs 53

Emotional Does Not Equal Illogical 54

CHAPTER 7

Isn't Technology Wonderful? 57

Communications, Galore 57

It Looked A Lot Easier on Television 64

CHAPTER 8

You Flew Him Alone At Age Five?:
Useful Information for Traveling and Children 66

Flying with Children 68

Unaccompanied Children and Flying 69

CHAPTER 9

The Tables are Turned 73

Oh My, They're All Gone! 73

Oh My, I Thought They Were Gone! 75

CHAPTER 10

Stories From Around 80

CHAPTER 11

Summing It All Up 94

CHAPTER 12

Handy Checklists 98

Medical and Emergency Treatment Information 98

The "Get-Around-To-It" List 99

What Did You Bring Me? 100

Flying a Minor Unaccompanied 103

Should I Take the Family Along? 104

When to Leave a Teen Alone Overnight 106

The Empty Nest as a Place to Visit 107

PART TWO—SOURCES AND RESOURCES

Background Facts and Studies 111

Department of Defense (DOD)
and the Military Services 111

Unofficial, But Service-Related—Plenty To Share 129

The National Long Distance Relationship
Building Institute 132

Parents Without Partners 134

A Woman's Focus 136

NOTES 141

SELECT BIBLIOGRAPHY 145

INDEX 149

Preface

Why This Book?

"Write what you know" is a long-standing rule, or in the words of Jimmy Buffet, "Don't try to describe the ocean if you've never seen it." I kept both versions of this thought in mind as I contemplated a topic for my first book-length nonfiction. While there are several subjects I can, and do, discourse on, I discussed the idea of *The Parent's Guide to Business Travel* with several friends. Their collective enthusiasm guided me into this effort.

There are, no doubt, parents in the world who are so adept at child rearing that they need no suggestions, and there are definitely parents who prefer to remain oblivious to emotionally sticky family situations. Many of the rest of us, however, can occasionally use a few words of advice when it comes time to deal with unfamiliar events. How to handle work-related family separations was not something I was prepared to do when I first faced the need to leave a toddler for several weeks. I could have used a quick reference in those days.

My initial plan for this book was to have a slim, stocking-stuffer-type publication, but the volume expanded as people would say, "Hey, did you think about adding. . . ." A variety of stories that came in in response to my invitation for the submission of personal experiences led me include some points that, no, I hadn't thought of, and I appreciated the comments.

In all honesty, an agent and a publisher both warned me that readers these days were only interested in nonfiction books by "experts with credentials"; to wit, someone with an academic title or celebrity status. I admit that I don't fit either category, so I sincerely hope that their assessment of readers is not correct. What I do have is nineteen years of fairly constant separations from the time my son was an infant through our current almost-empty-nest stage.

I'll talk more about my background later, but I think that *The Parent's Guide* will provide something of interest to any parent who has ever felt a pang of guilt, a stab of loneliness, or a surge of other emotions when he or she took to the air, ocean, or road and left the family behind. It is meant as a book that can be useful to new (or expectant) parents, parents whose children are entering new developmental stages, and grandparents and other relatives who may serve as caregivers to children when parents have to travel.

How the Book is Structured

Now, I know that not everyone reads the preface, so some of what I say in this part will be repeated in different sections of the book. *The Parent's Guide* is divided into two parts and then further divided into sections. Part One is for people who prefer to get right to the point and look for specifics. Part Two is the reference section, with some detailed background and useful information that will fit different needs, depending on your family composition.

A word about the websites that I discuss in Part Two. I have taken significant portions of text from several of the sites and used them verbatim. Readers who are comfortable with the Internet will know beforehand if it is a site they want to check out. I also hope that I will be reaching an audience that may either be unfamiliar with, or limited in access to, the Internet. In those cases, the large amount of text will provide enough information to give a good picture of what the site and/or organization is about.

A Mix of Tones

There was once a man who was very much in love with a lady and she with him. They were quite compatible in the ways that were important, but there was also the matter of a young son from a previous marriage. The man was concerned about his ability to enter a ready-made family and become a father with no preparation, and he voiced this doubt when an older friend of his inquired into the future of the couple's relationship.

"Do you think any of us know beforehand?" his friend countered. "It's not like you can take a course and get a degree that guarantees you'll be a good parent. Most of us just do the best we can and hope it turns out okay. If that's the only thing holding you back, then you need to stop worrying about it and marry the girl."

The man took the friend's advice, the couple wed, and to the best of my knowledge, the marriage and family are still doing fine.

Parenting can be serious business with wrenching moments, although, as the friend above explained, it is mostly just doing the best that you can. I have based this book on personal experience and written it from a positive view, notwithstanding some less-than-pleasant shadings in appropriate passages. I am fully cognizant that work-related separations can result in, or add to, family dysfunction, and I don't mean to make light of those kinds of problems. My heart goes out to parents and children alike who must find ways to cope with emotionally damaged relationships, and a book such as this is certainly no substitution for professional assistance.

The Parent's Guide is intended for the routine sort of ups and downs that come with hectic lifestyles in an increasingly mobile and globally oriented society that we Baby Boomers, GenXer's, and now the Digital Generation inhabit. I hope the ideas contained in Part One and the support organizations and helpful sites listed in Part Two will be useful for most families.

Brand Names, Not Endorsements

As an administrative note, there are some brand names of items or companies that I have mentioned throughout the book. I did so in order to provide specific information to readers, not in exchange for any commercial endorsement. I do not mean to imply in any of these references that the brands or companies cited are the exclusive sources for the services or items discussed.

Been There, Done That

I can no longer recall the origin of this wonderfully descriptive phrase. My juggling of career and family began with somewhat of a double whammy. My first husband and I met and married when we were assigned to Fort Campbell, Kentucky. I was more concerned with plowing my way through what was still commonly referred to as "This Man's Army" than with thoughts of motherhood, and so my pregnancy within six months of marriage (the details really aren't important) came as a surprise. We figured we could work through what were sometimes likely to be conflicting mission requirements; yet, four months after our son was born, my husband was killed in an accident. I had barely had time to get used to the idea of being a parent, and now I was instantaneously thrust into single parenthood in a profession that meant frequent relocation.

I was already on the path of a career in the Army, and I had no idea whether or not I would be able to continue with that or if I would be forced to admit that I couldn't meet the demands of service and taking care of my son. In an effort to be helpful, the Army gave me a two-year assignment to a post near my parents in a position that did not require field duty or deployments.

My son was three before I had to cope with yearly extended separations, and I was beset with more doubt than I generally acknowledged.

I used a mix of child care arrangements depending on where I was assigned: in-home daycare in one neighborhood; KinderCare and multiple babysitters later; and then Tammy, a young lady who lived with us in what was a mutually beneficial relationship. She forged a bond with Dustin that went far beyond basic child care.

I did remarry when he was eight years old, although marrying another Army officer didn't resolve the absentee parenting issue. In fact, our timing was pretty lousy. Eight months of being a family, ten months with my husband (and son's new stepfather) gone, two weeks together, six weeks apart when a housing shortage in Germany caused us to report for duty with Dustin to follow, four and a half months together, and then the Gulf War. Half a million U.S. military service members deployed as children, spouses, parents, and other relatives waited anxiously to see what would happen. I would be less than candid if I said my loyalties weren't strained between my duty to the Army and the country and to a ten-year-old child. I watched him and Tammy walk through the security gate at Frankfurt International Airport and did not know if we would ever see each other again.

We were reunited six months later with great thanks for a safe return. I can only assume that our continued requirement to periodically disappear for different missions contributed to Dustin's assurance that he, too, could travel on his own for purposes that suited him. Hop on a plane at age eleven and fly alone from Italy to Maine? Why not? Let's just say that if there were a prize for stay-at-home families, we wouldn't have been in the running. I do have to say that when Dustin was in high school, it *was* a bit amusing when people who weren't aware of our background would ask him if he was planning to go away for college or if he felt he should stay close to us.

Questions, Advice, and Those Pesky Unknowns

My husband has an undergraduate degree in applied physics, he reads *Scientific American* for enjoyment, and he can explain the difference between a quark and a subatomic particle. He rolls his eyes when anyone uses the term *science* in combination with something like *behavioral* or *social,* and looking at emotions under a microscope tends to be difficult for him. I have to agree with him that there are myriad, nonquantifiable variables when it comes to interpersonal dynamics and family relationships.

The ideas and feelings expressed in *The Parent's Guide* aren't meant to provide answers to all the questions that can emerge for parents and children who spend time apart because of business demands. Some of the tips will be immediately useful, some will be applicable at later stages, and some may not work at all.

The chances are pretty good, though, that somewhere in these pages, you'll run across a passage that makes you smile, gives you a good idea, or causes you to reflect for a moment. At least, that was the plan.

Acknowledgments

My acknowledgments usually require a couple of paragraphs, but I have a greater number of people to thank than usual for their contributions to, or support of, *The Parent's Guide*. I will do my best not to leave anyone out.

Nancy Merritt was one of the first women I interviewed, and I appreciated her candor. Others who shared stories and insight were Denise Bachman Dunn, Brenda Elliott, Marcia Enyart, Eileen Ledbetter, Carrie Lee (of Sgtmoms.com), Kim Joaquin, Joan Sugarman, Janet Truesdale, Beth, Dennis, Helen, Keri, John, Tonya, and several individuals who provided responses, but did not wish to be identified. Each of you added an extra dimension that strengthened this book.

My thanks also to Maria Bailey and Rachael Bender of Bluesuitmom, Aaron Larson of the National Long Distance Relationship Building Institute, Barbara Spade of Parents Without Partners, Janet Gilbert of Inova, Mount Vernon Hospital (Virginia), Ed Allen, the technology guy, and the staff at the Military Family Resource Center in Arlington, Virginia, for their quick response in locating the military studies cited in Part Two.

A special word of course for Noemi Taylor and Kathleen Hughes of Capital Books for their faith in this project, and for Margery Heffron and Eileen Delaney for their special care in copyediting and proofreading it.

A related thank you is important to those friends and family members who helped so much at times when I had to be away—my father and stepmother, Cliff and Mary Ruffin, my mother Mary Charlotte (no longer with us); my first husband's parents, Barbara Kimball and Dean (no longer with us); my husband's parents, Hughie Hudson and Foster (no longer with us); my sister-in-law, Leila Raines; my sister Gayle, brother-in-law Mike, nephew Chris; cousins Pam and Liz Pickett; friends Ann Smith, Joyce Teston, Kelly and Mike Redwine, Minnie and Dave McKenna; and Tammy, the marvelous young lady who substituted more than once as a mom.

My gratitude to Dustin, the son who understood the balance that I tried to achieve, and to my husband, Hugh, who has been a steadfast supporter in each project I have engaged in. I could never have accomplished the competing tasks without him. And a loving word in memory of David Kimball, Dustin's father and my first husband (no longer with us).

There have been others, of course, along the way who have given me encouragement and support, and I want thank them for that.

I also want to express appreciation to the men and women of family support organizations. While there are some paid positions within the many hardworking groups, thousands of individuals have given, and will continue to give, volunteer time to help parents, children, and other relatives cope with work-related separations. Thank you for your efforts, and thank you for the programs that have become realities and the networks that have grown because a handful of people were willing to take the steps necessary to take what was sometimes just a thought and nurture it into something more substantial.

And a word of thanks to readers, to those that I will never meet who support the dream of those of us who write—people who provide the two-way relationship that keeps the publishing world turning.

PART ONE

What, How, and Other Thoughts

CHAPTER ONE

Introduction

The Realities of Separation

You're in a distant city when you call home to say goodnight. Maybe you get the jabbering sounds of your ten-month-old who doesn't form recognizable words yet, or the plaintive question of your two-year-old who asks, "But, why can't you be here to tuck me in?" or perhaps it's the neutral, "Uh huh, I'm okay, " of your nine-year-old who wants to return to a favorite television show.

From the laptop-wielding road warrior to the individual who knows he or she can't move up that next rung of the professional ladder without being required to perform some travel in the job, business-related travel is a part of the working landscape. Electronic mail and reliable, high-speed video teleconferencing may reduce some of the need, but according to statistics maintained by the Travel Industry Association, business travel has increased by 14 percent since 1994 and is projected to continue to rise.[1] Despite the drop in travel after the September 2001 tragedy, approximately one-fifth of all working adults will take an overnight business trip at least once a year, and there is a reason that the number of extended-stay hotels such as Homewood Suites, Residence Inns, AmeriSuites, and others are expanding and thriving in the lodging industry.

Global connectivity, high definition video teleconferencing, and e-commerce are becoming more mainstream, but someone has to make the original deals with face-to-face negotiation, information sharing, and so forth. Although the 1990s economic boom that stumbled or stagnated in certain business sectors has slowed down many a company's expense accounts, travel continues to be key to a wide range of successful careers.

So what's the big deal? There have been parents who are business travelers for years, right? Absolutely, yet just as with the shift in other aspects of our social structure, the business traveler profile is changing and more importantly, the profile of the family left at home has changed. The average business traveler is still a married male, although the number of women travelers is steadily increasing, as is the number of single parents. The rise of dual-income parents and the "commuter marriages" that cut across several professional fields can sometimes result in both parents being on the road at the same time.

I spent seven years as a single parent and then married another Army officer. The innocuous sounding administrative label for the personnel records is "dual-service couple," but, to my son, it was a guarantee of more separations since his stepfather and I were both deployable until I retired at the end of twenty-two years. Dustin learned early on to cope with the idea of an absent parent, though the six months that my husband and I served in the Gulf War were, without a doubt, the most unsettling for him. While separations for military families do tend to be on the far end of the bell curve, the dynamics of having to be away are similar no matter what the profession.

I've written this book to explore those dynamics and offer some helpful hints on how to cope with the demands of your travel requirements and parental obligations to your children. It is divided by age groups since how you explain an absence to a toddler is quite different from what you tell an adolescent, and the rules you set when it's time to be away from the teenagers will be different still.

I've also included personal anecdotes from parents and young adults with their perspectives on the subject. I hope to provide insight and practical application for the parent or parents who must balance what can sometimes be guilt-laced, conflicting needs. While this book is not a social commentary, certain emotional reactions are a part of the package of family separation. Discussing those emotions is not something that should be avoided.

And in the vein of what this book *is not,* I want to very clearly state that I am neither a psychiatrist nor licensed counselor, although I have used several references written by individuals who are. I am an ordinary parent who, quite frankly, did not embark on parenthood with any thought of how to handle time away from my family before

I was faced with making necessary arrangements. For those who have the time and desire to delve deeper into the psychological and sociological aspects of developmental stages from infancy to adulthood, family relationships, or parenting skills, the references listed in the bibliography are excellent resources.

One of those references is Dr. John Gray's (the Mars/Venus guy) book, *Children Are From Heaven,* where he acknowledges the rise in writings about parenting. "Because of the invention of Western psychology, we are now much more aware of the profound influence childhood has on our success later in life. . . . Although we now accept this insight as common knowledge, fifty years ago it was not common. . . . With this increased knowledge of the importance of childhood, parents today feel much greater pressure and responsibility to find the best way to parent their children."[2]

The thought in the above passage is one of the reasons I included a chapter that touches on the question of whether or not you should travel and be apart from your family. I placed it later in the book because if you're reading this, I presume you already do, or expect to, travel. Whether or not, and *how,* your travel affects your family are issues that you probably think about and discuss with relatives, friends, or coworkers. The potential impact of travel is a subject of constant debate as well as numerous studies, and I would be remiss if I ignored the question completely.

A Word About Separation Anxiety

Not to begin on a negative note, but a quick look at separation anxiety is fundamental to dealing with many of the issues that arise when a parent travels. It is a reaction that begins in infancy before we have the capacity to understand what it is. The effects of separation anxiety can continue well into the teenage years, despite the fact that most teenagers would curl their lips in that disdainful way if asked whether they missed their parents. And let's get real about once we achieve adulthood—the millions of dollars in personal long distance telephone calls every year are not merely to help out the telecommunications companies' financial status.

The early cries of the baby who is picked up by someone he or she doesn't know, the worry experienced that first time you leave your child with a sitter, and the unsettled feeling you may have when you wake up in yet another hotel room away from home are all rooted in separation anxiety. It is a normal human response that varies in intensity and manifestation depending upon the individual. Age makes a difference, as does the manner in which it is handled. Recognition and management of that anxiety (for the child as well as the adult) is key for the parent who spends time away, and I trust you'll find a few useful tips in Part One.

ON THE OTHER HAND . . .

Looking forward to some time on the road is not out of the ordinary. The romantic getaway or the dream trip when your boss asks you to go to the meeting in Paris (or wherever strikes you as terrific), and you don't hesitate for a moment, does not mean that you don't love your children. And it may also happen that the kids have a lot going on in their lives at any particular moment and, maybe, get to overindulge in fast-food treats while you're gone, and it seems like they aren't concerned if you're not around. Those are the times that pretty much take care of themselves.

The purpose of this book is to discuss all those other times, particularly for the new parent or for those whose children have entered new stages, and what worked well in the past suddenly seems ineffective.

A Military Flavor

There are many professions that require frequent travel: the airline industry; the trucking business; the business of travel itself; certainly, any company that reaches beyond its home territory to another region, or outside our borders; and then there is the Department of Defense. Civilian employees and contractors associated with the Department of Defense may also be required to travel, but for the military members, it is a given from the moment an individual takes the oath of service, especially for anyone who spends more than one tour of service. Much of what I have written does focus on military families since that is my personal background and the area where I have the most access to information.

Operations Noble Eagle and Enduring Freedom are obvious examples of how quickly military personnel can go from routine operations to far-flung deployments. More than sixty thousand Reserve Component personnel (Reserve Component includes Reserves and National Guard from all branches of service) have been called to active duty to augment and support the active service members. Even before the War on Terrorism was declared there were U.S. military personnel serving in unaccompanied areas such as the Balkans, designated parts of South Korea, the Middle East, and regular six-month sea duty for Navy ship personnel. In addition to the tours of duty where families are not permitted, many service personnel choose not to take a family on an overseas assignment due to school, medical, or spouse employment considerations. As of September 2001, there were almost a quarter of a million service personnel assigned to more than 140 countries or territories and afloat.[3] (That number does not include the forces deployed and/or mobilized in response to the War on Terrorism.)

THE COMMERCIAL CIVILIAN SECTORS

"I think when you are in the military, you go into it knowing that it can take you away from your family, but when you accept a job that is in South Florida, you don't expect to be working in Denver," Maria Bailey, co-founder of Bluesuitmom, wrote in an e-mail.

Ms. Bailey's words were a great reminder to me (as were several conversations with my sister, who has a hefty Frequent Flier balance) that a military focus was fine as long as I didn't get overly service-oriented.

How the Book is Structured— Parts One and Two

This book is divided into two parts to try and make it an easy-to-read guide for busy people. Part One contains chapters One through Eleven and the checklists. It is basically the "how-to" portion. If you're in a hurry and just want some good ideas, you can pinpoint the age group you're looking for and focus on that piece, or you can flip over to the checklist you need.

Part Two contains reference material with background information and extracts of pertinent studies or reports. It is heavily weighted toward resources that can be explored to provide the next layer or two down into the complexities of parenting.

I decided to include extracts from some of the studies that the U.S. military has conducted and programs that have been subsequently developed because there has been a concerted effort since the late 1970s to assist military families, both Active Duty and Reserve Component, in coping with frequent or extended separations. The person who is new to the military often does not realize all the resources that are available to provide support and/or information, and perhaps this book can serve as an introduction to those programs.

The individual who is not associated with the military, but who also faces the same fundamental issues surrounding frequent and/or prolonged work-related separations, might be able to adapt some of the programs on a smaller scale. If nothing else, it can be interesting to know that this topic has generated a significant level of research.

Along those same lines, military-designed sites or organizations listed in Support Organizations and Helpful Sites in Part Two are certainly accessible to anyone online, and you should be able to get some good ideas from them. Additionally, there are several unofficial, linked sites that contain beneficial information or chat rooms for nonmilitary families. Bluesuitmom, as well as the sites of the National Long Distance Relationship Building Institute and Parents Without Partners provide information and support without going through a military site.

HIGH TECH HELP

I am not a gadget person, and it took me far longer to enter the computer age than I care to admit. I know there will be others like me who have limited ability or access to many of the electronic and communications devices that I discuss in Chapter Seven. My intent in this book is to provide ideas that are not tied to technology, but electronic means can, and do, make life easier in many ways. The constant search for newer, better, more advanced systems causes prices to drop and allows these items and associated services to become more affordable to a broader market. The primary reason the market has grown is because people are responding to increased communications/connectivity tools and services for family as well as for business applications.

STORIES FROM AROUND

As I mentioned earlier, a group of different people submitted comments and related experiences either through my website (charliehudson.net) or mailed in letters. Most of the submissions were from women and older teenagers or young adults, and there was an interesting mix of careers. While I did not get as many responses as I hoped when I began this project, the type of responses I received were rich with description and feeling. I was able to use all the submissions, although several people requested that I use their comments, but not identify them by name or location, and others provided no personal information. I wove many of the stories into the various chapters, but there were others that extended across multiple age groups or expressed overall emotion and/or philosophy about the impact of traveling.

These are the segments that make up Chapter Ten, and if you haven't found a part of yourself that you recognize in Chapters One through Nine, the odds are there will be something here that causes you to nod your head and think, "Yeah, that's familiar."

Come along then, and let's get started.

CHAPTER TWO

How Long *Is* a Week?
Infant to Pre-schooler
(Up to Age Five)

Infant to Toddler (Age Two)

Each age group presents unique challenges for the parent who must be away, but the youngest group is overlaid not only with a lack of the ability to communicate in sentences, but also with the fact that development occurs rapidly and continuously. The earliest that a baby seems to recognize a parent is still a matter of study, even though it is generally agreed that this certainly occurs within the first weeks. Then there are those momentous accomplishments of rolling over, sitting up, tentative, wobbly steps turning into mobility, first words being uttered, and so forth. These are events that new parents watch for, capture on film or video, and track against charts and tables.

This is also the period when parents may choose to alter their work patterns and/or make a concerted effort to avoid business travel. The longest separation may be a matter of hours when you finally decide to leave the baby with a sitter or child care provider—a decision that can be difficult for a lot of new parents.

I'll digress briefly from the primary focus to discuss the first-time separation experience because it is often a significant event and may set the tone for how you feel about future separations.

The tug-of-war between logic and your gut is often a back-and-forth contest with cognitive understanding of the qualifications of a sitter or day care provider on the one hand and nerve-wracking visions of a sudden fire or a baby gripped in inexplicable convulsions on the other hand. There is a tremendous amount of anecdotal data of the stomach-churning reaction and the tension of waiting for the telephone to ring to confirm fears that something terrible has occurred. Your disquietude can probably be eased with a reassuring call (okay, maybe there's more than one) back to the house. That doesn't always work, but for the most part, you'll be pleasantly surprised to find that the worry recedes, and you realize you really can relax and have a good time. Both responses are commonplace, and neither is intrinsically "good" or "bad."

If you discover that you worry a great deal, even though you appear outwardly calm, then you're probably not at the stage where you will be able to travel away from the child and concentrate on the purpose of the trip. It may be better to restrict your travel to perhaps nothing more than a short vacation when your infant is under the watch of doting grandparents or other relatives.

If you do find that you are comfortable with leaving your child in the care of someone else, you might want to try an overnight sort of situation where you can control the timing as a way to gauge your reaction before you plan a series of trips. A woman I know who is highly competitive and very business-minded was convinced that she was prepared to spend a night away from their six-month-old son when she and her husband attended a holiday function at a hotel and took the overnight package to give themselves a little treat. She was somewhat chagrined when she discovered that she couldn't relax and indescribably relieved when her husband said that her uneasy state of mind wasn't worth the price of the hotel room. They returned home to a peacefully sleeping infant, and her mother apparently wasn't the least bit surprised at their sudden change of plans. Several months elapsed before the woman was at ease with being away even for short periods.

While I went back to work when our son was approximately ten weeks old, and I did leave him for a week's stay with his grandparents at the age of eight months, I managed to avoid having to travel again professionally until he was around seventeen months old. That trip was also only a week long, and both of us handled it pretty well.

Most babies will not respond adversely to the occasional few days to a week's absence if they are in the care of someone they are familiar with. Naturally, that will sometimes be the very moment your son or daughter picks to suddenly perform one of those "firsts" you've been waiting for, but, if you're lucky, a camera will have been nearby to capture the event.

A critical point concerning separation during the early months is to minimize the degree of unfamiliarity that a baby is required to absorb at one time, since externally generated changes to a routine can be stressful. If you're the only one leaving, and your spouse will be in charge of the house while you are gone, then you may want to switch to whatever the new routine is before you depart. For example, if you're the one who always bathes the child, then do so together for a couple of evenings and then allow your spouse to do so alone for a couple of evenings.

If circumstances dictate that the baby will be moved to a different location, and the baby is attached to items such as a stuffed animal or other toys, then it's a good idea to have those items with him or her. Writing out the routines you have established may also help whoever is keeping the child, and if there is something in particular that you are concerned with, for example, you never leave a bottle in the bed at night, it's important that you write that down. On the other hand, it's equally important to remember that whoever is taking care of the child is not a clone of you. Mental alarm bells don't need to go off if you call and discover that bedtime was at 8 P.M. instead of 7:30.

If there is not a great upheaval in an infant's schedule, he or she will often seem less disturbed by the occasional absence than will a child between the ages of about fourteen to twenty-four months. The fear of abandonment is intense in young children, even though they don't understand this is what they're feeling. The child who has begun to speak will know that a parent is not around at the normal time, and he or she will certainly notice if someone different is in the house or if they are taken somewhere other than their home. The child may attempt to ask questions or "search" for you. Trying to explain "trip" isn't usually practical, although if you have shown the child your suitcase and said the words "trip" and "will come back soon" several times, it may be beneficial. If the child is already accustomed to you being gone to work on a regular basis, "work" combined with "trip" and a reassuring "coming home soon" is about the best you can do. A nightly telephone call at a regular time is often a good solution, and there are some other ideas in Chapter Seven.

A word of caution about your return, however, when children are at this age. You may be greeted with great enthusiasm, but it may also mean a bout of clinging or sullen behavior that takes you by surprise, especially if the child had behaved well until you came home. A show of temporary resentment or craving attention is not uncommon in very young children, and it will normally only last for a day or two. The quickest way to overcome what is basically confusion with your absence is to return to your standard schedule and repeat the phrasing of "work," "trip," and "home now." Each child progresses in comprehension of spoken words at an individual rate, and if you talk through why you were gone, it's possible that even a toddler may absorb more of the explanation than you think.

I am a firm believer in bringing back presents (more about that later), but if your child seems angry that you have left, you don't want to shower him or her with gifts and special treatment to make up for it. That can set a pattern in place that you will have a hard time sustaining or reversing later.

What should you take as warning signs at this age? Persistent crying while you're gone, a change in eating or sleeping habits that extends beyond a few days, a sudden dislike of your normal child care arrangements, and prolonged sulking when you return might be causes for concern. Again, most infants or toddlers are emotionally equipped to handle well-planned departures. If your child is exhibiting extreme distress, it may be an indicator that an effort should be made to avoid separations until he or she is old enough to adequately understand your absence.

And, of course, the flip side to the coin is you may find that the child appears to be coping well and you aren't. Difficulty in concentrating on your business, intense feelings of guilt, and elevated irritation with those around you may be a result of either the type of trip you're on or jet lag, but it's also possible that, despite your expectations, you discover that you aren't ready for time away.

My sister and brother-in-law were the first couple that I knew personally who spent some time in a semi-commuter marriage. My brother-in-law had completed his doctoral degree in chemistry and had taken a job in Houston, but my sister had several months remaining until she finished her doctorate and could join him in Houston for postgraduate work as a cell biologist. Their son was a toddler, and they made what was then the unconventional decision for my brother-in-law to take my nephew with him while my sister stayed in Iowa. They flew back and forth as often as possible during the separation. Both grandmothers went to Houston occasionally, my brother-in-law made all the other necessary child care arrangements, and while it wasn't easy for either of them, my nephew didn't manifest any extreme symptoms as a result. He did, however, have a tendency to refer to both my sister and airplanes with the phrase, "Airplane, Mommy, zoom, zoom, bye-bye."

Ages Three to Five

The ability to grasp the concept of "trip" is easier in these years, although understanding the passage of time will probably be limited; hence the title of this chapter, "What *Is* a Week?" Forging and maintaining a strong communication link during absences is important and can span from low-tech to the latest electronic gadgets—only the *means* of communication should change as your children advance in age.

A preschooler, particularly one who is in some type of child care arrangement, will become familiar with the idea of parents going to a job and will probably be comfortable with a statement that you have to take a trip to another place to do your job, but he or she can have difficulty with figuring out when you will return home.

By the time my son was three, we had made the first relocation that he could remember, and I was suddenly faced with an assignment that required me to be gone for nine weeks of the summer. As it turned out, this was to be the case for three consecutive summers. I was now eight hours' drive from where my parents lived and more than two thousand miles from my in-laws, nor could I see leaving a very active youngster with either of them for the whole period. [In case there's some confusion as to why my husband wasn't available, although I could depend on my in-laws, it is because my husband was killed in an accident when our son was four months old, and I remained very close to his parents.]

At any rate, after it became obvious that I could make child care arrangements for the summer or resign from the military, we collectively determined that I would drive my son to my parents where he would stay for three weeks, then they would fly with him to Maine and spend a few days with the second set of grandparents, who would keep him for the remaining time. It had been a tradition in the Kimball family that the children had summered in Maine in the country, so we were really just starting the tradition a bit sooner than usual. There were plenty of activities for my son to enjoy, he seemed to accept that I had to "go away on my job," and that left only the problem of trying to explain a stretch of nine weeks to a three-year-old.

Grandma Kimball quickly hit upon an idea that centered around "Cartoon Day." My son had designated Saturdays as "Cartoon Day" since that was the only day of the week that certain cartoon programs were aired (this was obviously before the advent of the Cartoon Network). It was a simple step to affix colorful stickers to each "Cartoon Day" on the calendar with a different sticker for the day they would pick me up at the airport. It was far easier for him to deal with nine stickers than what would have been a batch of sixty-three if there had been one for each day.

The second challenge was keeping in touch with my son and, while I called on a regular basis, a preschooler doesn't have a lot to say during a telephone conversation. I would send him cute post-cards or greeting cards with a sentence or two, although that first summer I wasn't aware of how meaningful those cards were to him. I missed a couple of weeks due to a very heavy workload, and my father said that one day when he went to the mailbox and pulled out some kind of advertisement that was on a colorful card, my son eagerly took it and said, "This is for me from Mommy."

My father picked up on the problem and heartily "read" my message of how I was very busy, but missed my big boy and hoped he was being good. Needless to say, I winced guiltily when I thanked my father for his fast thinking and didn't make that mistake again. What I did was buy a batch of cards, filled several out when I had some spare time, stamped them, and then spaced them out for mailing every few days. My son was too young to care what I wrote, and the messages were essentially all the same, but it didn't matter—he was getting "mail" from me that he could hold in his hand, and that was the important thing for him.

One of the other women whose daughter was about the same age as my son had more foresight than I did. She had tape-recorded a couple of her daughter's favorite bedtime stories before she left. That way, her husband, or whoever, could play the tape whenever the little girl wanted. Another option would be a videotape. There are far more technology tools these days, and the explosion of devices for keeping in touch is partially covered in Chapter Seven, "Isn't Technology Wonderful?"

The key point at this age is that, just like the repeated question, "Are we there yet?," small children do not distinguish segments of time well. It's crucial to find a method of counting days or weeks they are comfortable with so they can feel confident of when they will see you again. Otherwise, their question, "When are you coming home?" cannot be answered in a way they understand, and it will reinforce the frightening thought that you aren't really going to return.

This is also the age when it may be difficult to distinguish between imagination and reality, and a child may become fearful of something that doesn't occur to you. For example, if you have taken a trip to Arizona, but your child doesn't know where or even what Arizona *is*, he or she may conjure up disturbing images of you in a terrible place. Some children will blurt out their fears, while many will simply exhibit whining or irritable behavior. A few gentle questions that allow them to express their imaginings can soothe their worries.

One branch of my family is very close-knit, and three of the five children have settled near my aunt and uncle. The oldest daughter, Pam, has a marvelous ability with children, and for some time she provided in-home day care while she was also the primary child care provider for one of her nephews. An opportunity came up for Pam to travel to Italy to teach a prekindergarten class for two years, but the nephew was only three years old when she left. He struggled emotionally trying to understand where Pam had gone and why she wasn't coming home at the end of each day. Despite repeated attempts to explain the situation, he tended to ask, "Are we going to see Pam now?" practically each time the family got into the car. Pam called home fairly regularly, and she would start to speak with the child on the telephone, but when she would answer his question of "Are you coming home tomorrow?" with "No, not yet," he would refuse to talk to her. They tried maps and other approaches, but no one knew how to get the point across to him. Pam's sister, Liz, got a great deal on a flight to Italy, and she talked her brother and sister-in-law into allowing the child to accompany her. Once he made the transatlantic round trip, had a chance to see where Pam lived, and understood that she really was planning to return home, he adjusted to her absence. No one was ever quite sure, but they wondered if he had somehow concluded that Pam had decided to stay away forever and the grown-ups in his world were trying to hide that from him.

Nancy, a computer consultant and information systems manager, who volunteered to discuss her experiences, echoed the trials of communicating work-family balances to a toddler/preschooler. Nancy is one of those high-energy women who determined that being a single parent with a young daughter wasn't going to hold her back from making a better life for them both. She knew that the computer field was a place for growth and that one of the trade-offs for a progressive career would be an occasional trip away from her daughter. She limited her absences as much as was practical, and even though she could depend on her mother and her daughter's godmother to help, made the decision to move in with her grandmother for a period of time. This offered a workable arrangement for everyone and more stability for eighteen-month-old Brianne.

"For me, the large, extended family was definitely a key. There are too many things that can come up that you hadn't planned to have to deal with," Nancy said. "And if someone doesn't have a strong family base, I would think you'd have to seek out a support group. I can't imagine trying to cope with everyday events and traveling away from your family without something along those lines."

And speaking of things that don't necessarily occur to an adult— when I was talking to our son about this age group, he was quick to mention that it was easy for a child to assume a parent leaves because the child has done something wrong—something to cause the parent to want to be gone.

I was startled at his comment, but he said, "Hey, it's just the kind of thing that kids think of—that it's their fault, and Mommy or Daddy doesn't want to be around them. You have to be careful to explain that you wouldn't be gone if you didn't have to be. It takes a while to really understand when you're young."

After our conversation I searched my memory about the discussions I had with other parents, and I had to admit that it had never crossed my mind that Dustin would have entertained such a notion.

That meant I never addressed a concern that was apparently quite real to him at times.

Take this one step further, and consider how there may be occasions when you're either already stressed about taking a particular trip or pressed to get numerous things done before you depart, and you impatiently brush your child off. You can see that she might erroneously translate that reaction into a desire to get away from her.

Saying Good-bye

This can be a bit tricky and may change according to age group or vary from child to child in the same family. For some children, waving good-bye until you are out of sight or going with you to an airport can make them feel important. Others may want quick, undemonstrative departures. There isn't much way to predict this one, so it's probably best to do whatever you feel comfortable with, but be willing to adjust if required. You should think for a moment, though, if there are well-intentioned people who insist that a child behave in a "proper" show of farewell. If a child is disturbed about your leaving, you don't necessarily want to encourage a screaming fit, but you don't want to demand that he pretend to be happy about it, either. And if your schedule is such that you will slip away in the early morning hours, think about leaving something special for him to find in the morning when he wakes up.

How About Those Presents When You Come Home?

Ah yes, the "What did you bring me?" line known in advertising. I, personally, hold to the notion that a gift is a reasonable expectation, even though I also know there are others who would disagree. My son learned early on that the size of the present was directly proportional to the length of whatever trip I was on, and the nine-week ones were as good as having an extra birthday. Again, not everyone will use this approach, but I hold with doing what works for you. A suitable gift and dinner of my son's choice upon my return was the pattern for us. I distinctly recall one instance when I was to be gone for a week, and, in the discussion of what present my son wanted, he suggested that a Millenium Falcon (the first Star Wars series) would be perfect. I rapidly countered that it wasn't a "big present" trip, and without hesitation he switched his request to something smaller.

By the way, even though gifts are easy for young children, this can become "chore-like" later due to not knowing what to get or being pressed for time. There are a couple of fairly easy solutions to consider. One of the checklists I have included in the back of the book has a spot for clothing sizes and notes about hobbies or collections. It can be filled out, and you can carry it with you routinely, either in hard copy or entered into the handy computer.

Another option is the registry service provided by a number of retailers. While this was previously the domain of bridal gifts, many companies have adopted the idea for general use. Amazon.com has one of the more sophisticated systems. An individual registers and, at any point, he or she can add to the list. Since Amazon.com handles many items in addition to books, the "Wish List" can cover multiple areas. You can order a gift from the list, have it arrive when you do, and be reasonably certain that it will meet with approval. If you are not familiar with Amazon.com, it is one of the online companies that also provide express-type ordering, so you enter data initially, and their system retains the information to expedite future orders. The lag time between ordering and shipping may not be practical for short trips, but it can be nice for extended absences. There is a more detailed explanation of how this works in the checklist section.

And on the subject of presents—don't forget the spouse, other relative, or friend who has been handling the home front. Just think of it as an extra business expense.

A QUICK RECAP

Take note of how you react when you leave your infant alone with a sitter or child care provider for the first time—that will be an indicator of how you might feel about an overnight trip. Try and minimize the changes for your infant during your absence, and, if possible, make a transition to any new routines a few days before you depart to give the baby time to adjust.

Toddlers may experience confusion with your being gone, and telephone calls to them, as well as repeated statements that you will come home soon, should help. Your return may be followed by a bout of whining, clinging, or other expressions of anger. It's not unusual at this age and will disappear within a day or two.

Preschoolers will have a better grasp of the fact that you will be gone, but have difficulty in understanding a span of time, or their imaginations may conjure up scary thoughts about your trip. Find a way that *they* comprehend to communicate when you will come back, and pay attention if they seem concerned about where you are going. Keep in touch by whatever method makes *them* comfortable. Constantly assure them that your absences are due to work and not because you don't want to be with them.

Presents are a traditional part of homecoming, but don't get sidetracked into believing that it is the same thing as having you around.

Don't be embarrassed or disconcerted if you find that *you* are the one who has difficulty in coping with being separated, even if you think you are prepared for it.

CHAPTER THREE

You Really Should See The Pandas: The Older Child

The Elementary Years (Ages Six–Ten)

This age group has the advantages of enhanced communications skills and of understanding the concept of time. You will be able to more easily discuss where you are going and how long you will be gone. That also means that your children will be able to express feelings more openly and may have questions as to why you travel.

An interest in your travel will provide a good opportunity for exchange, and with older children, you may find that they enjoy seeing where you are going on a map or that they want to check the area out on the Internet. If your children are curious about the places you travel to, you might be surprised at the things they want to know if you give them a chance to talk about it. A good friend of mine attends an annual conference in Washington, D.C., and as she was discussing her itinerary, her eight-year-old daughter insisted that she make time to go see the giant pandas at the National Zoo. It seemed a strange request, but the daughter's class had been studying about the recent acquisition of the cubs from China, and she thought it would be a treat for her mother to see them. Fortunately, my friend was staying at a hotel near the zoo, so she was able to slip away for a quick visit. She snapped a couple of great digital photographs, e-mailed them to her daughter's class, and brought back a panda-emblazoned tee shirt. What a heroine Mom was from that trip!

School-age children often have fairly full schedules of their own, between what they do in class and other activities they may be involved with, so they may not notice your absence as much as they did when younger. The flip side to that, however, is that you now enter the stage when there might be programs or events that you are forced to miss. You may be able to control your schedule enough to work around such occurrences, but there seem to be universal forces that somehow collide to require your presence halfway across the country at the same time the fourth grade class is presenting its spring pageant.

The obvious solution is a video camera, although that only solves part of the problem if your offspring take your lack of attendance personally. One way to help alleviate the disappointment is to request a special family performance before you leave. Also be sure and telephone or e-mail after the event so you can be told about it. When you return, take the time to sit down, watch the video together, and receive what will probably be an animated commentary. The key is to remember that, no matter how often you say, "Of course, you're more important to me than my job," being willing to make this kind of effort helps drive the point home.

Working with your children to develop special collections based around where you travel is another thought. Magnets, posters, baseball caps, or other such items can be something enjoyable and can lead to shared discussions of the places that you go. These won't necessarily be things that are cherished for years, but they may well allow your children to feel more a part of what you do, and that, in turn, helps to keep them from feeling as if they are a lower priority.

How school is going will be another matter of concern for many children, and while you may routinely go over homework with your children when you're around, it may be comforting for them to know that you also care about that while you're away. E-mail is a potential solution, unless matching your time zone and/or schedule and theirs is too cumbersome. If long distance sharing isn't practical, set aside a half-hour or so after you get home to specifically discuss school and how things are going. That reinforces the message that you've been thinking about their world as well as your other business. Again, some children will have no interest at all in discussing school, but you won't know until you try. A word of caution though—the idea is to *listen* to what your children have to say—not to grill them about performance.

Another aspect of the elementary school years is that children pay more attention than you might realize to things they hear on the news. The intense coverage, thirst for live video footage, and broadcast of personal stories that surround airplane and other mass fatalities provide fertile soil for sprouting nervous reaction to the idea of those modes of travel. Events of September 11, 2001 have exacerbated the potential for fear among adults, and you may have been closely questioned by your child. Trying to explain the tragic day and its aftermath was difficult for most parents.

If your child does bring up the subject of travel being dangerous, don't dismiss it as nothing for her to be concerned about. Dr. Terri Apter provides this advice in the book *The Confident Child:*

> If a child exhibits anxiety parents, while meaning well, may dismiss what a child is saying as unreasonable. By doing so, this may increase the child's anxiety. This in turn may set a downward spiral into motion where the child feels unable to express anxiety. The aim should be to find a way to show that the anxiety is unrealistic and help replace the anxiety with a sense of control and confidence.[1]

A concern with flying is one of the best examples, even though it may not be the exclusive area of apprehension. On the other hand, if you, as an adult, are having misgivings or have altered your travel schedule for a while and then resumed travel, it is quite likely that your child will have noted the change in your pattern. You don't necessarily have to hold a family meeting to announce that you now feel able to return to flying, but you should be prepared to candidly discuss why you stopped and why you feel that it is okay to start traveling again. Rather than trying to explain that there's no need to worry, talk about the new security measures and why they are important. All right, enough of the heavy stuff.

One of the advantages of ages six through ten is that today's computer generation will be comfortable with e-mail, and if you're a laptop wielder, then you have a great link home that significantly "shrinks" the distance. If your child has an urge to "talk," yet he knows you aren't actually available, he can e-mail instead. Disparate time zones may prevent online chatting, but sometimes just the ability to send a message to you can do the trick. Of course, that makes it important for you to check your mail before you hit the bed at night. It only takes a few minutes to respond, and if you access your e-mail and find a hundred messages waiting, make those from your loved ones high priority and save the rest for later, if you're too tired to deal with them all.

There are a variety of high tech communications tools available on the market such as the desktop video screen and the instant-message link for e-mail. These can enhance the feeling of closeness, and I have listed as many of these items as I could (considering the rapidity with which they appear) in Chapter Seven.

Ah, Those Preteens (Ages Eleven–Twelve)

The "terrible twos" get a lot of press, but the changes your preteen experiences are the beginning of a hormonal, developmental roller-coaster that can rival anything you've dealt with up to this point. In a nutshell, this is an age where peer pressure tends to take hold, and if you can remember back to your own time (somehow, that's usually subject to a great deal of revisionism), then you'll recall that bridging childhood and the much-anticipated teenage world is filled with potential conflicts.

It may suddenly seem as if your children could care less if you're around or not, and like many families today, you may find that family time has virtually disappeared in the midst of work, school, and extracurricular activities. In this case, you might assume that your absence won't be noted—and you could be right—but it's not always as simple as that. (Right, as if *anything* about raising children is simple.)

If you traveled frequently when your children were younger, then, in one sense, it will be more of the same, and they are less likely to show much of an interest in where you are going, not to mention that, by now, they pretty well understand the obligations of your job. They may, however, feel your absence more keenly because they are subject to facing myriad "crises" in their lives, and they want to have you around whether they actually open up to you or not.

Drs. Stanley Turecki and Sarah Wernick discussed this issue in their book *The Emotional Problems of Normal Children* when they wrote, "Separation anxiety appears most often in pre-schoolers through first grade, but may re-surface at the start of middle school."[2]

If this does happen, try to get your child to discuss why she suddenly feels uncomfortable, rather than think, "Why are we going through this *again?* I thought we were past this phase."

Since this can also be an age when two-way conversation doesn't necessarily flow freely, you may be able to work through unarticulated anxiety by being open, yet positive, about your travels. Reflect that what you are doing serves a worthwhile purpose, even if that is only because it's a step in job progression that ultimately leads to something else that you want.

Preteens don't need to fix on career decisions, but this is a time frame when they can begin to understand that there are often conscious trade-offs that adults make. While most of us have been on trips that we would prefer not to have experienced, if you focus on the negative aspects, a preteen can easily be left wondering what the purpose of travel is. If you're miserable being on the road, or if that is how the child perceives your feelings, and the family has to be apart, they wonder if that is what they have to look forward to as a grown-up. (And by the way, if you *are* miserable on the road, maybe it's time to think about a career change. More about that later.)

On the other hand, if you delayed traveling when your children were toddlers or in elementary school, or if you subsequently move into a position where more travel is required, you're likely to go through some of the same first-time adjustments as did parents of younger children.

One of the women who provided input for the book, but requested she not be identified, brought this point up:

> I had taken the first four years off after our daughter was born, and then went back to work part time. I was able to arrange my schedule around a lot of her activities, but when she was eleven, I was offered an unexpected promotion in the company. It meant that I would have to make quarterly circuits within a fairly large region and would be gone for about a week each quarter. It was an opportunity that would have been hard to turn down, and my husband assured me that we should be able to avoid

being gone at the same time. For some reason, though, it just hadn't occurred to me that I hadn't actually been away from my daughter. I mean she had gone to sleepovers and things like that, but never to something like summer camp, and we always took family vacations together.

I went on that first quarterly circuit, and by the second day, I was surprised at how disconnected I felt. I'd eaten dinner alone in the hotel, I'd already called home, and here it was like at nine-thirty or ten o'clock, and it suddenly seemed like the next three days were going to last forever. I mean, I felt genuinely homesick, and here I was, a mature woman. My daughter had sounded fine, and my husband had said everything was okay, and yet, all I wanted to do right that minute was to be on my way home. I was stunned at how intense the feeling was.

Anyway, I know this is pretty long, but after I got home late that Friday, my daughter said it had been okay, just a little "weird" being alone with her father for the whole week. We talked about my trip and what she'd been doing, and she loved the earrings that I brought her. And that weekend we went out and bought a web cam set and signed up for instant messaging. That kind of traveling lasted about two years, and we all got used to it, but it was more disturbing at first than I had thought it would be.

You Missed Trash Pickup Day?

Another area that can come as a surprise to parents who travel is when regular routines they have established for the household are ignored during their absence. Perhaps it is something like the homework that doesn't get done at the expected time or, more likely, designated chores aren't completed. This can be viewed as the old adage, "When the cat's away . . . ," but the underlying truth is that many parents develop routines based on their preferences, and they expend more effort than they realize in enforcing those routines. Therefore, the enforcement is not available while they are gone. This is similar to what parents encounter with development in young children, in that neither the clock nor the world stops while you're on the road.

If you always insist that the laundry be done on Tuesday, the trash set out the night before collection, and the homework completed before the evening television shows begin, it may turn out that the laundry is forgotten until you arrive on Wednesday, or you call home and get asked a question about a chapter your child is reading while watching television. How a parent chooses to handle these typical situations is a personal matter, but it's important to understand that it should not necessarily be interpreted as an act of rebellion or passive-aggressive behavior. It's often nothing beyond that fact that a set of rules you consider essential to maintaining an orderly household is a view that's not held by all concerned.

If you find yourself frustrated by something of this nature, it's a good idea to think through how you really feel about the routine, rules, or whatever. If it truly bothers you, then you need to express that clearly and calmly and put certain checks into place when you travel. Perhaps you'll need to write out reminders, create some sort of checklist, or change the time when you telephone so you can either blatantly or subtly nag those at home.

Remember that this is the age of "in between" for your children—the threshold of being teenagers—too old for many behaviors and too young for others. This can also apply to how they feel about you traveling. They may miss you and think it isn't "cool" to say so, or they may indeed be involved with their own friends and activities and not notice much outside that sphere.

It is vital, however, not to assume that your absences have little impact, and some of the same techniques you used earlier are just as valid as during the younger years. Keep the lines of communication open, and if a telephone conversation stretches out in the telling you of some great event or an e-mail is waiting late in the evening, take the time to respond. If there are questions about where you've been and what you do during trips, use the opportunity to discuss work and career choices. Be the one to initiate conversations when you return home to clearly convey that you're interested in what occurs at home during your travels.

Speaking of Coming Home...

A celebration is likely to be in order if you've been gone for a long time; yet, there will be other instances when a child may want to make what seems to be a big deal out of a rather ordinary trip. This response can be due to several different reasons, but if a child asks to do something special or surprises you with an offering, then be supportive. Maybe she baked, or helped bake, a batch of cookies or created something on her own. Be sure to acknowledge her efforts, and remember that the next time you walk through the door, it may be to an empty house because everyone has gone off to karate class.

No matter what the age, though, consider having either a family dinner at home, or let your children pick a place to go for a meal out. You may be tired of restaurant fare, but it might be a special treat for them. A compromise approach is to take the family to a grocery store with a large prepared-foods section. Everyone can jointly select items for a meal that can be easily brought to the table, and clean-up means tossing containers in the trash. This way, if you haven't had an opportunity to eat in moderation, you can always opt for the roasted chicken and fresh salad, while others are going for macaroni and cheese with pizza on the side.

A family dinner, either at home or out, facilitates exchanges rather than making it seem like you're giving anyone "the third degree" about what may have happened while you were gone.

A Note for Single Parents

The nontraveling parent is the one who will be at home with the children in a two-parent family. A single parent must usually add the parameter of arranging for help, and in some cases, there may be multiple choices to be analyzed. Someone who can come to your house and keep the routines as intact as possible is probably the best solution, but this isn't always achievable for the adult involved.

Nancy, the computer analyst I discussed in Chapter Two, said her daughter developed into a very active and independent child, but as she became older, she reacted better to Nancy's travel when she was allowed to be in the decision cycle concerning whom she stayed with. Nancy admitted that she couldn't always accommodate her wishes, but was able to most of the time and was careful to explain the reasoning on those occasions when she couldn't.

I think the strangest set of arrangements that I ever made with my son during the single-parenting years was the time when I split his summer more than usual. My cousin, whom I discussed in Chapter Two, had her in-home child care business at that time, and it just so happened that she also met with some friends every weekend in a town not far from where my father and mother lived. Dustin also adored Pam (she really does have this incredible gift), so he stayed with Pam Sunday through Friday afternoon and enjoyed being around the other children. Pam would take him to a designated spot on Fridays, my parents took him from there, and then reversed the process on Sundays. This was the set-up for half the time I was gone, and then my parents flew with him to Maine where he stayed with Gram and Grandpa Kimball for the other five or six weeks. As I said, you have to be creative at times when there's no second parent available.

I also want to take a moment to mention that if you didn't happen to notice the entry in the table of contents, there is a segment on Parents Without Partners in Part Two. If you are not familiar with the organization, it is an excellent source to check with when you do have to think about how to handle new aspects of single-parenting challenges.

Taking the Family Along

For both the younger and the older children, you may sometimes opt for making a trip a family experience. According to 1998 statistics provided by the Travel Industry Association, more than thirty-two million business trips included travelers with their children. This can be a wonderful opportunity, and certainly resolves the concern of being separated, but it's not a decision to be made lightly. Expense is one consideration, but I'll set that aside and focus on the other key factors.

If there are limited activities in the area, or the facilities are limited, boredom may be a problem, and that will almost inevitably lead to crankiness. If your schedule is filled during the day, and you have required social functions in the evening, or the potential for supplemental meetings, then you'll have little time to spend with the family. On the other hand, if business takes you to somewhere like Orlando, or within a short distance of beloved friends or relatives, there should be plenty to keep everyone happy.

Another important factor can be child care, and what is actually available may not match what you think will be available. If on-site child care is a must for you, make sure you know what will be on the other end. Many large hotels either offer special programs for children of all ages or can arrange for participation in programs nearby. Metropolitan or resort areas may have businesses that market children's activities to organizers of conventions. Information about these opportunities can usually be found through the hotel, on the Internet, and through the local tourist office. If the hotel where you plan to stay doesn't offer a babysitting service, check the local directory under Child Care for companies that include temporary help. You may find an outfit like Mother's Aides, a Northern Virginia firm, that includes short-term, come-to-you assistance in their list of services.

Maria Bailey, one of the co-founders of Bluesuitmom (described in Part Two), mentioned that she often takes her children and combines a mini-vacation with work:

> The fastest growing segment of business travelers is women and there are many hotels now catering to these women, so they may bring their children along or stay over for a vacation. In fact, women business travelers are more likely than men to extend a business trip and take the kids as a mini-vacation. I did this last year during spring break when I needed to travel to LA. I took my seven-, six-, and five-year-old with me, and we went to Legoland and Knott's Berry Farm after my meetings had concluded. It was fun for me and they came to realize business travel wasn't a vacation for mom.

She directed me to the Wyndham Hotel website for information about their program developed with this market in mind. There is specific information from this site in Part Two.

The checklist in the back of the book, "Should I Take the Family Along," is a fairly inclusive list of the sorts of things you should work through before making the decision.

A slight variation of taking the family along is to have a child join you at the very end of a trip so the two of you can travel back together. This may seem mildly extravagant, but cost may be a secondary factor for you or you may get a travel bargain or redeem travel rewards. This method can allow you to share what will be an adventure for your child (particularly if he hasn't traveled much) during the part of your trip when you should be out from under work obligations and not have to divide your attention between your child and meeting agendas. So instead of rushing to make a flight after your last session, you can arrange to welcome your child at the airport, both of you enjoy an evening together, and then fly home as companions. If the flight is a short, direct flight, and you are certain you can be at the airport to greet the child, you can fly a child alone as young as five, although I wouldn't recommend this age unless a child already has experience flying. Most airlines will permit unaccompanied children to fly on connecting flights at age eight, but if you get into complicated flight arrangements, that can provide more adventure than either you or the child is prepared for. This may not be an option you want to exercise on a regular basis, but it might be something you haven't thought about.

"A FAMILY CONSTITUTION"

Joan G. Sugarman, of Washington, D.C., is a children's librarian and author of children's books. She sent me a delightful letter, in which she described the idea of a family constitution. Mrs. Sugarman raised five children and then had three additional child relatives left in her care. The concept of a constitution covers far more than the issue of work-related separations, but it can obviously be a component of what she refers to as "a pie slice from the whole of how to raise responsible, independent and whole children."

This particular approach is better suited for the older child, although when you read the mechanics of developing and updating the "constitution," it appears that someone as young as six could probably participate. I'm going to quote directly from her letter, and as you read it, you might want to adopt the entire idea or parts of it.

> May I suggest that one solution might be to write a family 'Constitution', with input from the children and with a weekly meeting guided by a rotating chairman from the family. Within it are guidelines for what is compulsory for the family's growth and living peacefully together, and a series of actions which enable the family to live peaceably and in harmony together. It will clearly state that there is a rotating chairman (footstools can be made lower or higher, thus enabling a small chairperson to be tall and 'in charge'). The family must agree to the components of the 'Constitution' and each have a copy.
>
> Changes can be made and voted upon for inclusion, along with comments or concerns verbally expressed at the weekly meetings. Guidelines

for living in peaceful harmony are based on honesty, consideration for others and the family needs and consummate direction. Purposes can be stated as they evolve from the membership of the family, i.e., living peacefully and in harmony together, identifying what is NEVER to be done along with specific guidelines by age level of what is expected from family members, and the usual cautionary examples of 'never done' activities, whether verbal or action oriented.

I realize this does sound strange, but now, five children later, plus three child relatives left in our care, I can only assure you that it works. Our five children today work mostly with women and children; two are doctors working with children, one is in charge of 'Head Start' in Vermont, one is a writer who has edited a newsletter involving blind children, and a fifth is an artist and musician and has worked for many years with children. Of the three children we raised, one works with special education needs, one is in communications and a third is an accountant.

When I left these youngsters for legal meetings, it took two persons to handle them while I fretted and worried about neglect of my child care obligations. Parents who need to be away learn how to trust their youngsters, but they worry nonetheless; freedom is endlessly enticing.

And you are correct in addressing the changing needs as youngsters grow. That is why a flexible Constitution is such a helpful tool. I even saved the one I made originally, in the early fifties, and it appears grotesque today. That is why constant modification and change were partners in its use. Family youngsters need to be heard in a courteous manner and input belongs to the entire family, as do many a decision, fortified by being in writing. The only constant is change, I suspect.

Parents who have to be away are merely one slice of the pie, or one veneer covering the problems. The base of it all is teaching responsibility, family standards of behavior and some kind of workable ethical code of family participation. The successful results are found in the children's feelings of self-worth, importance and their understanding of what is expected from them.

I had the pleasure of meeting Mrs. Sugarman not long before I completed this book; I found her to be one of those women devoted to the interest of children whether through literature, education, or simply by reinforcing the concepts of self-worth, combined with social and family responsibility.

Mrs. Sugarman's suggestion was an eminently useful structure for her family, but if you're not sure that it's right for yours, you could always give it a try and see. If it does become a good tool, that's great. If it doesn't, then maybe you and your family will have at least had an interesting discussion.

CHAPTER FOUR

A Different Approach For Teens

The tumultuous teen years are rarely uneventful for either parents or offspring, and this is the time when issues of control can escalate with unsettling speed. It is perhaps more important than ever to realize that if you travel a good deal and try to simultaneously maintain tight control over the household, you'll need a significant level of energy. Does that mean all bets are off and you should allow chaos to reign during business trips? No, although there may be moments when that's what it feels like.

If you've already encountered the bombardment of parental decisions that come with the magic number thirteen, you can easily tick them off on your fingers—dating questions, clothing choices, music preferences, learning to apportion time between school and extracurricular activities, the trauma of a driver's license, and, sometimes, the sudden recognition that the train will not slow down. The baby that you thought would never learn to speak in sentences is now fully capable of what can be eye-opening conversations.

If the influence of friends has been fairly low-key up until this point, the odds are it will gain strength rapidly. The telephone calls you used to make home may be met with a constant busy signal while the line is tied up with either teenage talk or the computer is online; and the gifts you bring back will now probably be the wrong thing. And somewhere in the midst of these changes, you're likely to hear,

"Well, I'm old enough to stay by myself, you know." Now if *that's* not a sit-up-and-take-notice phrase, I don't know what is, but it does raise a question that I'll address later in this chapter.

Adolescence First (Ages Thirteen and Fourteen)

Dr. Lawrence Kutner, in his book *Making Sense of Your Teen,* contends that the adolescent years are the least understood of any developmental age and therefore often result in more tension within many families than is expected. I found the following passage to be particularly applicable:

> Researchers have found that the frequency of parent-child battles has two predictable and related peaks. The first occurs during the *terrible twos,* when children are struggling to demonstrate their physical and, to a lesser extent, emotional independence from their parents.
>
> The second peak occurs around the time of puberty. These struggles also revolve around independence and control. Of course the arguments with adolescents are different from those with toddlers or even school-age children, for teenagers can use them to test their newly improved, but imperfect skills at reasoning.
>
> Although they may at times act as if they have little use for their parents' opinions and guidance, teenagers are desperately seeking help in understanding the world from their new perspective.[1]

Laura Sessions Stepp, a mother and Putlizer Prize-winning journalist, delved deeply into the lives of a small group of adolescents in her book *Our Last Best Shot: Guiding Our Children Through Early Adolescence.* The following is a part of the introduction:

> Early adolescence is our last best shot at preparing them for a successful life. It is not our last opportunity, of course; our children's intellectual and emotional growth continues for years afterward at a slower pace. But it is our last *best* opportunity because they are beginning to adopt patterns of thought and behavior that will accompany them for years to come.[2]

Joseph P. Shapiro penned an article in 1995, *Teenage Wasteland?* that emphasized distinctions about this transitional age. In the first part of his article he pointed out why "early adolescence is one of life's trickiest transitions."

> Adolescence is a distinctly American and 20th century notion. It was psychologist G. Stanley Hall who, in 1904, first proposed that there was a stage to life other than childhood or adulthood. But Hall painted a gloomy picture of adolescence, particularly early adolescence. He called it a time of sturm und drang, or storm and stress, for hormone roiled kids. The best thing adults could do was to get out of the way and let kids' rebellion pass.
>
> Even the physical changes that mark adolescence are coming sooner. Puberty occurs two years earlier than it did a century ago, apparently the result of better nutrition. Young teen's mental and physical growth is enormous.
>
> Young adolescents develop abstract reasoning, giving them their first adult skills for decisionmaking.[3]

The idea of trying to ignore this phase, as Dr. Hall suggested, will be more tempting as you approach the threshold, but Ms. Stepp's concept of taking this "last, best shot" is far better, and, hopefully, more productive. The bottom line is that, while the degree of emotional and developmental upheaval will vary from child to child, you need to be prepared for a genuine difference between an older child and an adolescent.

If you've already forged an understanding of why you travel and where the family fits in the priority list and have established solid communications, that may mean your adolescent will take your absences as routine. Yet, even if you have a firm foundation and nothing in your adult life has altered, communications can become strained, or at least tested, as Dr. Kutner said. It is vital for your teen to know you're available to discuss topics such as what extracurricular activities should be pursued and the vexing realities of physical changes. You may not receive lengthy telephone calls or e-mails while you're on the road, but these are the kinds of subjects you'll need to be cognizant of during the time you're at home. A short, one-week trip for you may, conversely, be filled with turmoil for the adolescent, whose whole world can be affected because of an impending social event. Your willingness to listen and/or give advice can be long distance or in the same room, but accessibility to you is the key.

The Core Teenage Years
(Ages Fifteen–Eighteen)

Post-high-school decisions to be made, first loves, driving licenses, cars, and other assorted issues enter the family scene at some point during these phases. If you have somehow managed to delay major battles or had only low-level skirmishes about independence until this stage, then you need to brace yourself. It is possible, of course, that you will be one of those parents who have established such an unshakable relationship with your teen that you will encounter few bumps in this segment on the journey to adulthood. For the rest of the population, however, this can be a period of rocky adjustment.

While your absence might seem to be less keenly felt during this time (other than if your presence is desired at a significant event), the control issues may well be more intense than ever before. Additionally, you may find yourself at a point in your career where you're required to increase business travel either due to job requirements or because the perception is that you're available for travel since you no longer have young children at home.

The peaks and valleys of teenage landscape aren't insurmountable obstacles; they're more like slippery pieces of emotional terrain that you need sturdy walking shoes and good balance to negotiate. How much control you wish to exert while you are on the road will depend on your personality, but if you find yourself in continued conflict with your teen, perhaps you need to reassess the areas of conflict. Dr. James Dobson had this to say in his book *Parenting Isn't For Cowards:*

> Pick and choose what is worth fighting for, and settle for something less than perfection on issues that don't really matter. . . .
>
> The philosophy that we applied with our teenager can be called "loosen and tighten." By this I mean we tried to loosen our grip on everything that had no lasting significance, and tighten down on everything that did. We said yes whenever we possibly could, to give support to the occasional no. And most importantly, we tried never to get too far away from our kids emotionally.[4]

As an added note to this chapter, there appears to be an interesting trend in that many parents (exact figures have not been compiled) are opting to cut back on travel as the children get older. This is the reverse of the parents who chose to stay close to home with infants and toddlers. The idea for these parents is that fundamental child care is obtainable for the early years, but the situations facing today's adolescents and teenagers are serious enough to warrant being more available at this stage. Peter Jensen of the *Baltimore Sun* staff interviewed a number of Baltimore area parents and his March 2000 article covered this option. All of the individuals that Mr. Jensen described in his article explained that mistrust of their adolescents and/or teens wasn't a consideration; it was a desire to be present physically. As one woman recounted, "It's not like a kid wants a parent to be on top of them during adolescence. But I can't tell you how many conversations took place with my own kids because I just happened to be there at the time when they felt like talking."[5]

Once again, this specific choice is highly personal and depends on a variety of factors; yet, it may be a viable one for your situation.

On the other hand, if your teen grew up with you traveling, it is quite likely that he will consider himself as more independent and self-sufficient than his peers who have little experience with a parent or parents who are often away. And if you take a moment to genuinely think about what you've asked your child to do in the prior years—"Now be a big boy/girl. Don't be childish, you know Mommy/Daddy has to travel"—then, isn't that feeling of independence a trait that you fostered? If so, then it logically follows that your teen may want to exert his ability to handle the home front on his own.

Home Alone—If and When

Notwithstanding the Macaulay Culkin movies, you might want to rent a copy of Tom Cruise's first big hit, *Risky Business,* if you are entertaining the idea of allowing a teen to be alone during an absence. While that might be an unfair benchmark to use, there are numerous factors that enter into such a decision. The primary ones are the neighborhood you live in, the level of maturity your teen possesses, and the length of time you will be gone.

The first time our son announced that we didn't need to worry about making arrangements for him was when he was on the brink of his fourteenth birthday. Due to one of those quirks in military life, both my husband and I were required to participate in a multi-day war game that would include missing our son's birthday. Since we were in Hawaii, and the exercise was being conducted in Fort Lewis, Washington, we explained to Dustin that we didn't share his view. We were living on Schofield Barracks in what was admittedly a safe and controlled-access place, but we were also scheduled to be gone for nearly ten days. My husband's executive officer, Dave McKenna and his wife, Minnie, lived about a mile away in another area of the post. They offered to have Dustin stay with them, and he reluctantly agreed that if we insisted on supervision, the McKenna household was a good place to be. We compromised by permitting him to leave there early each school day and walk back to our house to shower, dress, and catch his regular bus. It was a bit of an odd set-up, yet it worked all the way around, and Minnie, bless her heart, went out of her way to make Dustin a special birthday dinner complete with chocolate cake and photos for us.

The arrangement worked so well that I was taken aback when a mere four months later my husband and son decided to experiment with the asserted independence. I was deployed to Haiti for Operation Uphold Democracy, and my husband had to go to the Big Island (Hawaii) for two days. The rationale on this occasion was that the trustworthy neighbors promised to be available if needed, and it was a short period of time. Actually, everything went smoothly, no disaster befell, and the two male members of the family wisely didn't mention the plan to me until after the fact.

So, when did we make a conscious decision to permit our son to be alone in the house à la Tom Cruise? Twice, or maybe it was three times, during his senior year of high school. We were in Virginia by then, in a nice, quiet development, with neighbors on either side of us that we knew and trusted, the absences involved no weekends, and I made afternoon or nightly telephone calls at unscheduled times. Dustin had his own car, school was just a few miles away, his only extracurricular activity was martial arts, and he solemnly swore he would limit visitors to the usual suspects. Am I absolutely certain that nothing occurred that would have distressed me? No, but if something did happen, it wasn't noticeable to the neighbors, and the house was still clean and relatively uncluttered when we returned.

The best advice that I can offer if or when you face this question is to assess the pros and cons carefully. If you decide to allow overnight independence, make sure you have a good safety net of relatives or neighbors that you can call on and then truthfully evaluate the results when you arrive home.

The checklist in the back, "When To Leave A Teen Alone Overnight," is a quick way of reviewing the pertinent points. While I developed it primarily for parents, it might be useful to have your teen go through it independently to see how he or she responds to the questions and considerations. If they are able to satisfactorily address all the issues, that would be an indication that they have a reasonable grasp of the situation.

Remember Though, They're Not Adults Yet

This isn't really a throwaway comment. I learned a long time ago that every now and again, you *do* have to state the obvious. Most parents aren't going to consider a fourteen-year-old as anything but that, but a seventeen-year-old may exhibit characteristics of maturity and responsibility that can cause a parent to forget that lapses into childish judgment may still periodically occur.

There are also those cases where children grow up far too fast, and at thirteen or fourteen, have been placed into roles where they do behave in a way more suited to someone several years older. This can be especially true in a single-parent home. A poignant e-mail was sent in by what I am assume is a young woman, although the individual may be older and reflecting about her experiences from years before:

> I saw a note about this book, and I felt that I had to write, but I don't want to tell you who I am. I was twelve years old when my mother ran off with this guy and left my dad, me, my little brother and sister. We were all really ly shocked and it was awful, but I know part of the reason was because my dad was gone lots, and I think my mother just got fed up with it. The thing is that he was, I mean, is a good man, and I know he loved us and maybe just wasn't paying attention. I knew my mother cried a lot, and when I was ten, she started leaving me at home to babysit and was going out with some people to bars and places like that. I didn't really understand what was going on, and maybe I should have told my dad, but I don't know if it would have changed anything.

The thing is that after my mother left, someone had to take care of my dad. He stopped having to travel for a while and then started back again. My school wasn't very hard, and I made good grades without having to study much, and I already knew how to cook and pretty much had been doing the laundry and stuff like that, and my brother and sister had their jobs they did around the house. My aunt and uncle and cousins lived on the next street, and if we needed something, we could go over there. I was really mad and upset with my mother and in looking back, I suppose that I didn't want my dad to think he needed to find someone else to take care of us.

The remaining part of the young lady's e-mail described the role she took on as the substitute mother and housekeeper. The trade-off, as often happens, is that her life as a teenager ended with the acceptance of adult responsibilities. She reiterated that it was the right decision for her and her family, yet she also realizes that she did miss out on normal school events that others participated in.

It is an unfortunate reality that there are thousands of households where adolescents and teenagers begin to shoulder parental-type duties beyond routine babysitting or chauffeuring for siblings. Sometimes adults recognize the burden on the teen and sometimes the transformation occurs without anyone genuinely understanding what has taken place. Parents who travel a great deal need to be sensitive to the fact that they may inadvertently send a message to their adolescent or teen that they *want* him or her to assume an adult status when it is neither actually desired and certainly not appropriate.

Notwithstanding family situations such as that related above, a teenager who possesses a high degree of natural or situational-produced independence will have far fewer problems with coping with a parent's absence, but that doesn't automatically mean that it won't matter. A sense of loneliness and wanting to have a parent available can settle over the most well-adjusted teen.

I'm not implying that a teenager who seems comfortable with one or both parents being gone a great deal secretly harbors resentment and disappointment. I just think that it is important for parents to remember that teenagers will usually be reluctant to express feelings of missing a parent. How do you tell the difference? The signs tend to be there if you pay attention. Direct questions are an approach, although the, "Is something bothering you?" is often met with a "Nope/no/naw/nu-uh," answer.

Teenagers aren't children, but neither are they adults, and their dissembling skills are not usually finely honed. Follow-up communication is not as difficult as many parents imagine even though packaging it in a nonquestioning way may be required. Family dinners, even if only once a week, are a great reminder that you *are* a family unit despite hectic schedules.

If a teen inexplicably lingers around the kitchen/study/den talking about things that don't appear to be related or have *a point,* this is frequently a desire to either work up to a particular subject or perhaps to see if you are willing to take time for him. And as surprising as it may seem, you should remember that every now and again, your teen can enjoy talking to you just because they do.

CHAPTER FIVE

Hey Mom, My Arm Is in a Cast! and Other Worrisome Thoughts

Sooner or Later

Of course, you're afraid this will happen someday, and the first step is fairly simple—stay calm. We faced these kinds of calls three times—two that were relatively minor, and one that had me in tears—but each situation had the common element of dealing with disturbing news in a long-distance capacity.

The first event was at the tender age of six and a half and involved doing a trick on a swing set that had been accomplished several times successfully, so my son made the reasonable assumption that he was one step closer to being an action hero. The subsequent fall and chipped elbow surprised him, and it took a while for his grandfather to notice the swelling. By the time I got the call, Dustin was far more interested in describing the procedure he'd gone through to get the cast than he was in explaining what had happened. Well, okay, he never actually explained, but I did finally get him to let me speak with his grandfather. Now, I admit that Dustin's cheerful reminder that it was his left arm and he was right-handed helped convince me that my presence was not required to provide maternal care. It was, nonetheless, somewhat disconcerting, and I would have no doubt changed my schedule and been on the next airplane if his grandparents had indicated they needed the patient taken off their hands.

The shoe was on the other foot for the second, far more serious, incident. I had remarried, although we had had only nine months together before we were faced with a ten-month separation (standard fare in military families). We were fortunate in that the separation was due to a professional school and, therefore, only halfway across the country so that we were able to see each other approximately every six weeks. My husband and I were in between scheduled visits when Dustin became ill with what I, and the clinic, mistakenly thought was strep throat. The meningitis manifested itself later in the week, and the distressed look on the clinic physician's face as she called for an ambulance was enough to send my heart into overdrive. The doctors in the emergency room at the hospital briefly questioned me about the sequence of his illness and moved swiftly into action with a spinal tap to relieve the deadly pressure on Dustin's brain. I must acknowledge that I became utterly weak-kneed as I watched the procedure.

I didn't completely stop trembling until they transferred Dustin to a room in isolation and hooked up an intravenous antibiotic. I maintained enough composure to return to the office to inform my boss (who immediately told me to get back to the hospital and not worry about work) and my deputy and to bring a little calm to our live-in sitter. I held together while discussing his case with the school nurse, and, by then, I knew I would be able to reach my husband. I got through "hello," and then spent a few minutes sobbing into the telephone, which wasn't the kindest thing I could have done, but I needed a shoulder at that point, even if it was fifteen hundred miles away.

Dustin was officially out of danger and, according to the military rules, that meant my husband had no grounds to return home for the six-day hospital stay. He called every day to talk, and I understood it was difficult for him, knowing that I was working half days, "sleeping" in the recliner in Dustin's room every night, and there was really nothing he could do to help.

The third emergency room occasion had to do with appendicitis, and, once again, I was the one who got the telephone call, but the principles were the same—ascertain the level of risk and work through the desire to drop everything and rush to my child's side.

I was in Italy, and Dustin and my husband were still in Germany, due to join me in less than a month. I was already booked on a flight to see them at Thanksgiving, and based on my husband's report of Dustin's condition, I waited the two days to make my trip.

The inflammation had been caught virtually at the onset, and there were no complications to either the operation or recovery, but there's just something about a conversation that begins with, "Well, it wasn't exactly just a stomachache, and they're prepping him for surgery. . . ."

This *was* one of those times, however, when I began to give some thought to changing to a profession that wasn't quite so blasé about expecting the at-home parent/caregiver to cope nonchalantly with non-life-threatening illnesses. The truth be told, I suspect my husband and son felt the same way.

I'm still not entirely sure if making or receiving these types of telephone calls is the most upsetting, but if the moment comes to you, the two most important points are: a) find out what the real story is; and b) say to yourself, "This is not my fault" several times until you mean it. Contrary to all those sentences that you might want to start with, "If I'd/you'd been here/there," that will rarely be the case. Simply put, accidents and illness occur in the normal course of life.

I was shocked by the meningitis incident, and during the speeding trip down the highway behind the ambulance, I berated myself for not having returned my son to the clinic sooner—surely, I must have missed some kind of sign. One of the doctors on the team took time after they had stabilized Dustin to speak to me quietly and firmly:

"You didn't do anything out of place," he said. "Unless there have been other cases of meningitis in an area, it's not the first thing you think of. Don't put yourself in the position of panicking every time your child runs a fever and has a headache."

In all fairness, though, you do need to remember that the spouse or caretaker will have nursing tasks added to their schedules and this may be a legitimate cause to shorten your trip. Anyone who has ever been on the receiving end of a comment like "Well, it's all fine and good for you to be out of town while I'm dealing with a sick child" knows what I mean.

Thinking Ahead Won't Make It Happen

An illness that begins with a runny nose treatable with over-the-counter medication and then escalates into something like bronchitis gives you some reaction time. The accident or sudden high fever and swollen throat that occur in the early morning hours may require quick action. That will not be a pleasant time under any circumstances, but it can be especially stressful if the parent who has to react is the one who doesn't usually deal with medical matters. The Medical and Emergency Treatment checklist covers the basic information, and a checklist should be filled out for each member of the household. The easiest solution is to keep a central folder or file and have the location of the file in an easy-to-find place. If you keep a list of emergency numbers near a telephone, for instance, this is an ideal spot to note where the medical information file is also. I know this is one more thing to add to your plate, but once it's done, it doesn't usually change much, and it is of incredible value when the need arises. If your child attends school, you would have filled out something similar, and you may have been required to provide an annual update. You can always keep a copy of that form at the house, although also having directions to the closest hospital and the doctor's office is still a good idea.

This becomes even more important if you travel and your child is left with a non-parent. It is absolutely vital to keep a power of attorney updated and to have the family physician, known allergies, current medications, and medical insurance information easily available. A power of attorney is a quick, inexpensive document that can be obtained through most notary publics, and many workplaces have legal offices that will prepare them at no cost.

Family physicians will not normally require documentation, and if it is a true emergency that results in a trip to a hospital, medical personnel are authorized to take minimal life-saving measures when minors are involved, even if you have not provided a power of attorney to a non-parent. Most places will attempt to contact the parent or legal guardian before administering treatment, but notification takes second priority to treatment. There will, however, be follow-on paperwork, and inadequate documentation only serves to complicate what will be an already stressful time.

Medical and doctor information includes dentists, by the way, since children seem to have a penchant for breaking teeth almost as much as bones, and, oh, can those braces be fragile!

I don't mean to be alarmist, but another often-overlooked medical factor is blood type. Many people don't think to request that a child's blood type be determined as a routine procedure, but if that information is needed during emergency treatment, medical personnel will have to stop and perform the test before they can proceed. I had always assumed that Dustin shared either my or his father's blood type, but that wasn't correct. This was a case where a recessive gene kicked in, and he isn't anywhere close to being O Positive.

But broken bones and appendicitis aside, even a minor sore throat can cause a child to request tearfully that you come home and make her feel better. The fact that a dose of medicine, a cup of chicken soup, and a night's rest should have the same effect may not be met with understanding if your child is in one of the younger age groups. If you truly can't break away, or your spouse or caretaker tells you it really isn't necessary, then you might want to send an extra treat like a balloon bouquet or a kid's bouquet with a small stuffed animal.

How about canceling a trip to care for a sick child? It may be appropriate, but if a child is unhappy about your departure and thinks that a tummy ache can keep you at home, you might want to thoroughly assess the actual medical condition when the moans begin.

Then again, if your child seems to develop a variety of maladies that coincide with the times when you travel, it could be stress-related. While everyone thinks of stress with something like an ulcer, there are in fact, numerous ailments that can be due to, or be magnified by, separation anxiety. Some allergies can be affected; gastrointestinal problems and the onset of insomnia are other conditions that can emerge and not necessarily be immediately linked to stress. All of these can be treated, but if the root cause is stress, the problem is likely to recur unless the underlying concern is resolved. If a child is physically affected by separation anxiety, he or she may not be aware of the connection because of unconsciously suppressing the feelings of anxiety or actively trying to hide them. There is no reason to automatically think there is a relationship, but if there is a noticeable pattern, consult a physician about the possibility.

CHAPTER SIX

Should I Be Traveling Anyway?
The Debate Continues

Opinions and Studies Abound

This is neither a question that can be answered with a one-size-fits-all response nor a debate that is likely to be resolved anytime in the near future. It is an issue that has received increasing attention since the late 1970s, and it is not my intent to add to the noise. What I hope you will take from this chapter is that there are some serious issues to consider, yet there are also many variables that can affect each family's situation.

When I was in the early stages of this book, a woman I was talking to said the title should be "Not By Choice," a reference to her experience of frequent separations while she was on active duty in the military. As discussed in earlier chapters, the training and real-world deployments may not be familiar to individuals without a military background, but the woman was correct in the sense that there is little choice for those who serve. A situation that interferes with a service member's ability to deploy is grounds for dismissal, and all single parents and dual military couples with children must have an approved child care plan on file to designate who will take care of their children in the event of a separation. This is one of the reasons many service members do not remain in the military for a full career, and it is a standard factor taken into account when predicting turnover. While the military has initiated a number of family-oriented programs to help mitigate the effect of separations, deployments are an unchangeable part of service life. It can pose difficulties, and I don't personally know a single leader who has ever faulted a service member for citing this as a reason for leaving the service.

There are fewer structured, mandated restrictions in the corporate sector, and it is a relatively simple matter to change jobs with short notice, but the financial or prestige implications are likely to be greater. Numerous jobs are explicit about their "road warrior" aspect, and if you want to succeed in that venue, you will travel extensively. Then again, some travel-heavy professions are front-loaded in that the on-the-road demands are early in the career path, and you are later promoted to behind a desk, so all you have to do is hang in until that time. Does that mean that if you accept a position when you know there will be significant time away from your family, it's a "bad" choice? And, if in traveling, you can provide more for your family, is that "better" for them?

There is no shortage of studies, opinion pieces, or talk-show transcripts to support both sides of the issue, and conflicting conclusions can often be drawn from the same study. Opposing parental anecdotes and myriad pronouncements from "experts" are added to the mix, and it is little wonder that this question is pondered by millions of parents and parents-to-be. Part Two of this book contains extracts from several studies and reports. The selected passages in this chapter speak directly to the twin sides of guilt and resilience.

Dr. Irwin Matus specifically addressed feelings of conflict in his book *Wrestling With Parenthood*, where he wrote, "A note of painful realism: To some degree, the problem [insufficient time] is not solvable. Competition between needs and agendas is inevitable, and it is unrealistic to expect that conflicting schedules will always be resolved in favor of the children. The scarce resource of the parents' time must be distributed in the most equitable and workable way."[1]

Balance Doesn't Always Mean Equal

Ellen Galinsky, president of the Families and Work Institute, echoes the key point of equitable distribution of time in a comprehensive study that was the basis for the book *Ask The Children*. This inclusive work was published in 2000 and directly addressed issues such as time spent at work, availability when a child is ill, involvement with school and other activities, the level of communication between parents and children, the effect of work-related stress on home life, and the perception of how finances entered the picture.

Part of what makes *Ask the Children* unique is that the basic study entailed surveys and interviews conducted with 605 employed parents with children age eighteen or younger and 1,023 children in the third-through-twelfth grades. Ms. Galinsky's book focuses on the relationship between working parents and children in general rather than on the single aspect of parents who must travel away, but much of what the children say can be equally applied to the subject of absences.

Ms. Galinsky has been involved with various studies since the mid-1980s, and she is cautious about the constant quest for the "definitive" answer about the impact of work and children.

> As you can see, our national debate about working and children has been conducted as if the answer is either yes or no, as if one path is inherently good and the other bad. But more than four decades of research has shown that reality is not so simple. Outcomes for children *depend* primarily on what parents do with their children when they are together and secondarily on what happens to the children when they are away from their parents.
>
> There is also an either/or notion of balancing work and family which has been endlessly promulgated in books and other media. Balancing connotes a set of scales. If one side is up, the other side is down. The goal, as working parents typically see it, is to keep both sides even or equal. Although the notion of balance is correct in considering both work and family on the same continuum, the connections are more dynamic than balance implies. Both sides can be up and both sides can be down. What works for one person doesn't work for another.
>
> Finally, there is the concept of quality time versus quantity time. This concept implies that *either* the amount of time *or* the quality of time is more important. Yet, as you will see, this study of parents and children makes it very evident that one can't separate the amount of time from what happens during that time.[2]

The closing pages of Ms. Galinsky's book carry ten messages from the children's perspective—ten messages that carry a fairly straightforward theme to adults:

1. Work if you want to work.
2. We are proud of you.
3. Love us, raise us well.
4. Keep on working and supporting your children.
5. Spend focused time and hang-around time with your children.
6. Put your family first.
7. Be there for your children—or else.
8. Don't bring the stress from work into the home.
9. Find out what is going on in your children's lives and tell them about yours.
10. Teach your children how to work.[3]

The theme of the children was that they understood work is necessary, either from an economic and/or personal achievement point of view, and they didn't mind that, but they didn't want to be pushed aside and made to feel as if they weren't a priority in their parents' lives.

Is this the sort of conflict that Dr. Matus referred to? Absolutely, and the simple fact is that finding the workable distribution of time will normally require a deliberate effort. This, by the way, is not merely a statement of the obvious. It is meant as a reminder that you cannot create more hours in the day or days in a week just by trying a little harder.

If travel is a significant part of your job, in either the number of trips taken or the duration of trips, the effort required to share time may be easily exacerbated. Cindy Loose, a staff writer for the *Washington Post*, wrote an article for the paper in May 2001 in which she discussed the guilt factor for many parents. "But my angst, and the angst I believe she [her daughter] hides, is not unique. Studies are in short supply, but anecdotal evidence abounds." She acknowledges that despite her concerns, her travel schedule isn't likely to diminish soon, and adds that she does what she can to ease the burden on her family when she is away.[4]

Dr. Matus covered this point later in his book: "While children are vulnerable, they are also adaptable and resilient. In small doses, adversity can have beneficial results. Its function is to help develop resistance to the stresses of life. Without some adversity a child remains vulnerable to the tests that will surely come later in life."[5]

A book by Anne and Herman Roiphes, *Your Child's Mind: The Complete Guide to Infant and Child Emotional Well-Being,* echoed a similar thought specifically aimed at the impact on younger children:

> Because the baby reacts to the separation, it does not follow that the parents must never leave home. It means, rather, that the number of separations should be kept to a minimum and the care of the baby while the parents are gone should preferably be done in the baby's own home to eliminate some of the changes. It means that mothers in particular should expect some anger when they return.
>
> Family life is made up of a thousand compromises; there are imperfections from the point of view of all members. It is, however, better for the baby to have parents who are contented with each other and their own lives than to have parents in constant attendance who are depressed or bitter or bored.[6]

The statement "Your children grow up so fast, you know," cuts both ways. It is an absolute that you cannot turn back the clock and regain time that is spent away from your children when they are young. The opposite side of that coin, however, is that your children will grow up and have lives of their own. If you bypass career opportunities solely because you thought that it was in the best interest of your children, were they actually better off?

Having suffered my share of guilt pangs concerning whether or not I was allowing my career to inappropriately affect my son, I spoke with some seventeen- to twenty-two-year-olds, whom I knew had experienced frequent and long absences from parents. I was genuinely surprised at their responses. I admit that I used a fairly small sample for this book, but they all voiced the perception that they had adapted quite well and felt no lingering effects of neglect. In one specific situation, I had empathized with a friend of mine who had spent months worrying about being gone to Korea for a year when her children were ages ten months old, three, and five, respectively. When we asked her seventeen-year-old daughter how that year had been for her, I was certain she would talk about a feeling of abandonment, yet she more or less shrugged and said it had been okay. "Well, you wrote and called a lot, and the presents were neat," she said when we pressed her for more detail.

I confessed to my son and one of his cousins that I found this across-the-board view to be different from what I was expecting, and they looked at each other in a knowing way before Dustin said, "Well, Mom, we're a lot more interested in what's going on now than when we were kids. I mean, you did what you had to do, you were always good about explaining it, and you made it as easy as you could. It was just one of those things."

I absorbed what he said, as I bit my tongue to keep from reminding him of the petulance he'd exhibited at a younger age, because I realized that he was right. That *was* how he felt at the time, and he couldn't have known then that there would be more important things on his mind when he was older.

This position would seem to support the Roiphes' passage, Dr. Matus's comments, and Ms. Galinsky's findings and will, I hope, help salve the level of guilt and/or anxiety that many parents feel. Children do react emotionally, and there is a better than average chance that, at times, they will be angry because you have to travel, but they are fully capable of understanding at a later age that your absences were a necessary part of your job.

The catch is, of course, that you must make your decision based on the present, and the outcome can't be known until after the decision is made; sometimes, long after. The next two sections may help you sort through some of the potential warning signs and the powerful emotions that can weigh into the process.

Warning Signs

Missing an inordinate number of events in your children's lives, stress-related ailments that affect you or other members of the family, a prolonged lapse in communication with your children, a noticeable decline in your children's academic performance, experiencing the feeling that you can't cover all the bases, or that you don't really know what's going on at home are strong indicators that perhaps you should consider cutting back or eliminating travel for at least a while.

There may well be career consequences if you shift track, but that will very much depend on the company that you work for and on what your aspirations are. If you do find that you feel the need for a change, check closely into company policies to see if options like telecommuting or job-sharing might be available. The upper strata of the company might be out of reach with such a decision, but will they actually be *in reach* if you don't change?

A very dear friend once took an assignment that was considered a "career killer" in lieu of one that was usually a stepping stone to the next rank. A number of people were shocked, but he privately told me that he had never planned to stay in the Army beyond twenty years. His career successes had simply led people to assume that he sought promotion beyond what he did. He made his final, "off-track," assignment choice not only because he had consistently spent time away from his family, but also because he didn't want to "block" the assignment from an individual who really did have that kind of career potential and desire. Naturally, rumors floated about that his subsequent retirement was due to his unwise choice of jobs, but he shrugged away the talk for the inconsequential patter that it was.

Another example is a friend of mine who had been promoted to a point where she was unhappy with the increasingly bureaucratic nature of the position. The larger salary and perks also meant nearly 30 percent more time on the road. A reorganization within the company resulted in the offer of some early buy-outs, and she nervously took the deal. It did mean a drop in pay initially, but the buy-out enabled her to cover the gap as she developed some other contacts in a related field, and, within less than a year, she was working a more flexible schedule with almost no travel and making an equivalent salary when she discounted the work expenses she had previously incurred.

Emotional Does Not Equal Illogical

A very long time ago when I was a lieutenant with little thought of marriage and less of children, I received a piece of advice from a boss that I have evoked more than once. I'm not going to get into a lot of detail, but we had been out for a field exercise in nasty winter weather, and a number of things had not gone according to plan. I was scheduled to take leave and go visit my family, and the boss and I were discussing the exercise in order to tie up loose ends before I left for ten days. I was disappointed in my performance, and I was also approaching the completion of my initial commitment and could resign from the Army if I chose to do so. As our rehashing of events trailed off and my boss was double-checking the dates that I would be gone, I mentioned that I might look into civilian employment while I was home. It sounded like a pretty terrific option considering how the past few days had been.

My boss nodded and said, "Well, that's okay if you want to. This business isn't for everyone, but right now, you should go home, take a hot shower, eat a decent meal, and get some sleep. Don't ever make a decision to quit when you're cold and tired and feeling stupid."

It is not that his statement was unique, but it is easy sometimes to allow emotions to sway a decision. It can be tempting to say, "Okay, that's it. I'm going to stop being on the road so much (or at all)," if you have been on a frustrating trip, if the child/children are complaining about your absences, and/or your spouse injects some extra guilt. That could be the correct choice to make even though a hot shower, decent meal, and good night's sleep might alter your perspective.

Conversely, not everyone is suited to separation, and it is not irrational to vote with your heart. A woman who worked as a Department of Defense employee and declined to have her name used sent in the following:

> One of my children was only two weeks old when I had to leave for a trip. It became a constant in my job, and in the early years of my children, it could be up to one week every month. I know that my husband and the other relatives remaining at home were taking excellent care of the children, and I would always call them either before bedtime or before they went to school in the morning. I would bring them a small token home and tell them how much I loved them, but for me, as a female parent, the guilt and the thought of, "am I doing the right thing" never went away. Part of the reason I quit my full time job was the guilt of absence.

If you have taken the steps to ensure that your children are cared for while you're gone, if you have discounted the disgruntlement of travel arrangements that go awry and tedious meetings with boring or obnoxious people, if you know you are good at your job and the money is nice to have, and you still would rather be at home than on the road, then that is quite possibly the right choice for you and your family.

Otherwise, make whatever arrangements suit your personal situation, keep the communications link open, try to be gracious if well-intentioned friends or relatives think you should stay home more often, pack your suitcase, and let the experts continue to conduct their studies.

CHAPTER SEVEN

Isn't Technology Wonderful?

Communications, Galore

The recurring theme about establishing and maintaining two-way communications has been undeniably brought to the forefront due to the sheer availability of communications options. An older woman who had managed a household with four active children and a husband who was rarely at home clucked her tongue when we were talking about coping with separation:

"I admit that I sometimes get impatient when I listen to wives these days," she said. "I know the issue of family separation gets a lot of talk, and when I listen to women carry on about staying in touch, I just sort of shake my head. I know that expectations have been raised with the ease of communication devices, but thousands of us had to learn to cope with long periods of complete silence back during Korea and Vietnam. We had four children, and my husband had five tours to the Far East. You were lucky when you got letters, and long distance telephone calls were scarce. And I suppose the fact that we were all athletic helped keep us busy. Everyone was on two teams because they were very seasonal then, and you didn't have basketball and baseball overlapping. By the time the children put in a day at school, spent time at practice, and we attended each others' events, I'm not sure they thought much about missing their father.

My husband and I came to an agreement early on that he would focus on his career, and I would handle the family side, and after he retired, it would be my turn. Maybe that wasn't the most conventional thing in the world, but my husband wasn't one to spend a lot of time talking about emotions, and he certainly wasn't cut out to feel guilty for putting his career first. I don't know, maybe it suited my character better, too. The children and I had our own routines, and when he was home, he was smart enough not to try and change things. He sort of moved in and out without disrupting the flow. And I admit that I was very careful not to make comments about his absence as a drawback, even when things went wrong. We just managed whatever the situation was and made the best of it. If our children felt neglected, I couldn't tell it. Of course, I do think many husbands today participate more in childrearing, and I imagine that can make their absence more difficult in a way. We didn't have the tools for staying in touch, so not using them could hardly be an issue.

This chapter is centered around the *tools* part. It is not for the *digital edge, can't wait for the next cool toy to come out of research and into production* person. It is written instead for those who have trouble figuring out how to program the video recorder or for people who dabble in electronic gizmos, but don't necessarily turn to the technology magazines for entertainment. It is essentially a primer and quick review of the most accessible items on the market as of this writing.

I want to emphasize that the items, services, and technologies in this chapter are what was available at the time I finished the manuscript. There are constant changes in the price and type of personal communications services that are offered, and equipment that was on the drawing board suddenly appears on the store shelves. The most important point of the following pages is to provide a fairly plain-language explanation of the types of communications tools that ordinary individuals can use in everyday lives.

TELEPHONE, PAGERS, AND FACSIMILE MACHINES

The proliferation of cellular and digital devices has reduced the cost, and perhaps increased the confusion, of what is available, but all plans allow for expanded regional or nationwide calling at a monthly flat rate. The basic rates have a limit on minutes in most cases, yet the number of minutes has been significantly increased for still under $50 per month per telephone. When shopping for a telephone plan, it is important to ask how many telephones are covered in the plan. It is usually one, although special promotional offers may provide for additional instruments at no, or reduced, cost. You should also ask about monthly fees and taxes. It is not uncommon to pay 10 to 18 percent for such costs, and that is never printed in large type in the advertisements. Also check to see what the restrictions are for the minutes. For example, the minutes included may be only for certain hours of the evening or for the weekends. If you travel in different time zones, the great deal may not apply to the times when you want to use the minutes. Also, be very clear about the geographic area of coverage. If you rarely travel outside a specified region, nationwide calling may be a service you won't use. Sometimes these rules will be spelled out clearly, but make certain that you ask the direct question.

The new telephones are often equipped with voice mail and may have features that include the ability to leave short text messages so a family member can indicate the essence of the call. "Miss you, please call" may not be right up there with "The XYZ deal has been clinched," but for the child who wants reassurance that you can be reached by keying in a message, it *is* important.

There are usually at least five or six competing plans at any given time, so when you decide to take one, or upgrade your current plan, your best bet is to gather all the information at one time and do a quick comparison for cost and benefit.

Basic questions to ask are:

How many telephones do you need? Does a region cover enough area or do you need nationwide instead? Which of the features being offered will you actually use? (Three-way calling may sound like a fun thing to have, but how often do you do that?) How long is the contract period for? Will the plan allow you to upgrade periodically? (Some will as they offer new rates and telephones, and some will force you to cancel the current plan and apply for a new one.) Does the plan allow for rollover minutes if you have some left at the end of the month? (Most don't, because they would rather you take the largest number of minutes available for the greater cost; it's just good business on their part.)

The "Dick Tracy" wristwatch telephones with the miniature picture screen are not quite available yet, but you can bet it won't be too long before they make an appearance, even though you can expect a hefty price tag at the first offering.

Home facsimile (fax) machines are commonplace, with a starting price of around $200, and don't require a separate telephone line, although a second telephone line may be well worth the cost. Installation of a second line varies, but you can expect to pay $100 or less, with a $10 monthly fee. Many new homes and apartments already come equipped with two (or more) lines, and your local telephone company may have periodic special offers for multiple lines. Children who can't read or write can draw a picture that can be sent by home fax or receive a picture and/or note from a parent. Most of the major hotel chains have either on-site business centers or fax machines in the rooms. This is an easy alternative if you don't have a laptop computer or you don't have remote access to electronic mail.

A FEW WORDS ABOUT COMPUTERS AND STAYING CONNECTED

The power of computers has increased even as the cost has decreased, and although desk tops systems now range from $700 to $3000, most of the connectivity tips described in this chapter will require systems in the $1000 and higher bracket, depending on how cutting-edge you want to be. The available hard-drive space, processing power, ports, and multimedia capability will all be factors to consider. Laptops run from $1100 to $3500, with the more powerful ones essentially like desktop systems.

It will be important for you to discuss your connectivity desires with an expert, and what you may want to do is purchase an initial system that can be expanded to accommodate more features at a later date. You can find expert advice at any of a number of computer stores, with an independent consultant (usually listed in the telephone book or other local business advertising sections), perhaps at your place of business, or you can call one of the build-to-suit-your needs computer companies such as Gateway or Dell.

ELECTRONIC MAIL (E-MAIL)

As commonplace as e-mail is, there are constantly changing features to enhance its use, and you may not be aware of some of the new programs available for very young children. The following items range in cost from minimal to high end:

Basic e-mail (for those who may not be familiar with it) is provided through some sort of Internet Service Provider (ISP), and, again, there are usually several providers competing for your business at any one time. Most plans cost a set monthly fee (anywhere from seven dollars and up), and that buys a certain number of online minutes per month, and then there is a separate charge for additional minutes. Many people opt for the slightly more expensive plans that have unlimited minutes. Unlimited minutes usually run ten to $12 and up, per month. It will be important though to know if you will be sending mostly text messages or if you expect to send attached items such as photographs (more about that later). Some ISPs do not handle attachments well, and even though they might provided reduced rate plans, you won't have the capability that you need. This is one of the specific details you will need to ask about, and if you get a garbled answer like, "Well, it depends on whether you'll be sending HTMLs or JPEGs or. . . ," stop the individual and insist that they respond in terms that you are comfortable with.

There are some devices you can buy that will allow you to have basic e-mail without having a computer, even though a computer is required for many of the features that you probably want. Also, you can buy hand-held instruments like a "BlackBerry" if you don't want to use a laptop. These cannot accept attachments, but do take basic text. A larger device is the "Mail Station," which is laptop or desktop. The instrument is similar in size to a keyboard and costs approximately $50 to $100, with a monthly service charge of around $10 with unlimited e-mail. After the account is activated, you unplug a telephone line, insert it into the Mail Station, and you're ready to send or receive e-mail. It works with text only, but does not require a computer.

Additionally, many business centers in hotels, airports, and companies like Kinkos have computer time available for a fee where you can check and send e-mail as long as you have an access number through your Internet Service Provider. Your ISP customer service representative can arrange remote access.

OTHER E-MAIL AND INTERNET FEATURES

Instant Messaging—This is the kind of e-mail feature that you see on television advertisements and in movies like *You've Got Mail* where two individuals "talk" or "chat" back and forth on a computer. While in one sense it's the same as being on the telephone, many people find it to be a fun way to communicate, and instant messaging often comes at no extra cost with your Internet Service Provider. Both parties do have to have the instant messaging feature and both do have to be online at the same time, but those are the only requirements. It can also be a good mechanism for discussing homework.

Web Cameras and Video Conferencing—Web Cameras and video conferencing. Web cameras are the small cameras that are affixed to a computer and allow for individual or group conferencing. They are fairly easy to install, although, again, both parties must be available and online at the same time to communicate. In actuality, you'll have a web camera, software, speakers, and a microphone, but speakers and microphones come as included equipment with many new computers so that all you have to add on is the web camera and software. Basic web camera set-ups start at around $100, but the price ranges into the thousands of dollars for the more sophisticated, full-fledged video conferencing capabilities. Web cameras and video conferencing are great ways to feel closer than instant messaging, but unless you have a high-speed connection like the DSL and the more expensive equipment, you won't normally get the sort of big-screen transmissions that you see in television advertisements. Again, consult with an expert, and be realistic about what it is that you want. A simple face-to-face, small image will probably suit your needs.

Digital Cameras and Video Cameras—Unless you're gone for extended periods of time, these may be of more use on the family end, but it can be a terrific project for your children to make photographs and/or movies to e-mail to you by way of computer. Digital cameras have dropped dramatically in price to as low as $300 with the upper ranges still $800 to $2000. The lower priced cameras usually have a card interface capability with your computer instead of a disk inside the camera. Some companies also offer a "dock" for less than $100. You place the camera into the dock and tie into the computer that way. Digital video cameras now weigh only one to one-and-a-half pounds, although the price runs $900 to $2000. If the price seems a bit high, it can always be a good family Christmas present. Some video cameras may require special software or cards that cost about $100 more. Analog video cameras, however, are down to $400 to $800. While the images aren't as sharp as the digital, as long as you have the proper connections, you have the ability to make home movies. Cameras are readily available in the electronic departments of major stores as well as camera stores, although you will want to talk to someone knowledgeable to make sure you get the features that you want. The most important point, however, is to make sure you have compatible capability in the computers that you plan to use to send photographs or videos through the Internet.

There are two other options when it comes to e-mailing photographs if you don't want to buy a digital camera. The first is to buy a flatbed scanner for $100 to $200 and upload the images to your computer that way. The lowest tech approach is that most photo developing places now offer an option to have the photographs printed on a disk as well as on paper, and you then e-mail, using the disk.

MP3 Players—One of the latest high-tech gadgets that kids love for playing music is the MP3 player that operates with compact disks (CDs), but you can also use a memory stick for recording something like reading a series of stories. To us baby boomers, it's a new version of the cassette recorder, but it's much more "cool" for the digital generation and can be ideal for a child who can't read yet. You can either prerecord the stories on the stick before you leave or create recordings when you're on the road to then transmit by computer. All you need is a microphone for your computer, the memory stick, and the proper connectivity to both computers. You speak into the microphone where the data is then converted, stored, and is ready to be sent through the computer to download on the other end.

COMPUTING FOR YOUNG CHILDREN

The digital generation accepts the high-tech communications gadgets as routine. Ed Allen, of D and E Consulting and Repair, helped me with this chapter. He chuckled a bit when I asked him about children and computer skills and said that kindergarten through fifth grade is the best time to teach them. As he explained to me, the major obstacle for children tends to be keyboarding, and the computer industry has responded by creating software designed for ages eighteen months (yes, *months*) to three years. The software is specifically aimed at getting children comfortable with the mouse and the keyboard, although random key access is often incorporated. This means that the child can press any key, and the program responds. It allows the toddler to become accustomed to the keying motion even though correct key-to-function knowledge will have to be developed at a later age.

One software package is *Jump Start for Toddlers*. It has one version that holds a scrapbook that will enable a child to create drawings and/or it can incorporate digital pictures. This means that even a very young child can "draw" a picture for a parent who is away and "send" it over the computer. Just think of it an as update on the crayon or finger-painted drawings that adorn refrigerators the world over. Another program, *Naturally Speaking*, goes a step further and helps guide a child through keyboarding with a series of icons and voice commands.

These and other similar programs can be a wonderful opportunity for parents to sit down with a child and learn the programs together in preparation for separation, and then basic skills can be built on this early foundation.

It Looked a Lot Easier on the Television

"That's not fair," I protested to my husband the first Christmas we were married. The large, interactive, flashing beam toy that Dustin wanted came practically assembled. The contraption was ready and sitting under the tree in less than twenty minutes. "It doesn't count unless there is a missing piece or the instructions don't make sense."

"It helps if you have an idea of what you're doing before you get started," my husband said with a smile.

All right, I am not visually oriented, and that, by the way, is a valid reason why some people have genuine difficulty with following written directions. It has to do with the way the brain processes information. I need a clear picture of how the pieces go together rather than text instructions and a two-dimensional drawing with lines crisscrossing "Tab A to Slot D with Inset X," or whatever.

A flashy advertisement on television and a quick demonstration by a sales person who has repeated the same motions dozens of times won't be much help after you have gotten home and are stumped as to which connector goes into what slot, and why do you have an extra piece of cable?

Electronic and digital products will not be beneficial if you don't know how to use them or know who to call if there is a problem. Most of the items aren't that scary once you get used to them, but many of them do require several rounds of practice and fairly frequent use. The six-year-old who wants to send a picture on the computer will probably bounce around asking annoying, rapid-fire questions as you dig out the instruction book and try to remember which button to push.

If you are the parent who is the more technically inclined, don't become enthralled with these terrific systems and then exasperated when the spouse or caregiver on the other end hasn't a clue how to make the thing work. Be patient with those of us who really *can't* understand those stupid instructions and write things out in a step-by-step way, and practice with the gadget beforehand, and accept that yes, you have to explain it one more time. Or at least make sure that the eight-year-old next door will be around to help.

CHAPTER EIGHT

You Flew Him Alone at Age Five? Useful Information about Traveling and Children

This chapter serves two purposes. First, I have discussed a number of situations in the previous chapters that entail children traveling in some capacity, and, second, one of my cousins asked me to. There are some great books that are devoted solely to the subject of completing a trip with everyone's body parts and mental stability intact, and I have listed a few of them in the bibliography. The areas that I cover here are just some key points to keep in mind.

Traveling with young children can be particularly challenging and logistically cumbersome, so in the finest tradition of capitalism, dozens of products such as built-in changing pads in diaper bags have been created specifically to ease this part of traveling. Practical, reasonably priced items can be found at family discount stores, or you can wander the aisles of the high-end stores, surf the Net, or flip through the pages of catalogs for new offerings. Essentially, keeping children fed and entertained are the keys to smoother trips, no matter what the mode of transportation. The only thing I will say about feeding is it's good to remember that salty foods will lead to a greater need for drinks, and that tends to lead to the need for more frequent bathroom breaks—just a fact of nature.

As for entertainment, you can choose from traditional, no-equipment-necessary games like "Twenty Questions" to the virtual explosion in portable entertainment systems available to fit almost any size pocketbook. Good earphones are a must for entertainment systems in vehicles. Aside from safety concerns of distracting the driver, a friend of mine once forgot the earphones when she launched on a fourteen-hour drive with her grandson. By the time they arrived in Florida, she thought that "Barney" should join the ranks of extinct dinosaurs.

VEHICLE TELEVISION-VIDEO SYSTEMS

Primarily designed for minivans and other vehicles with vertical space, this television-video player combination usually runs around a $1000 option for new vehicles. Separate systems can be purchased in a range from $400 to $1000 and installed by any shop that specializes in vehicle sound system installation.

DVD PLAYERS

Another option is the stand-alone, portable DVD player with a range of $900–$1500, although major electronics stores may discount them by 40 percent or more. Additionally, most laptops now offer a DVD player option.

LAPTOPS

Even if you don't have the DVD option, you can have the full range of laptop uses in a vehicle, as long as you remember that battery power will be important for long trips. You can purchase a power cable that will fit into a cigarette lighter for around eighty dollars and there are also solar battery rechargers in the $75–$100 range, if you want to cover that possibility.

GAME SYSTEMS, AUDIOBOOKS, AND MUSIC

The technology of portable games systems is solid, but the drawback is that many games tend to evoke verbal exchanges, including potentially loud outbursts, so you might want to focus on music and audiobooks instead. The choice of audio players covers the spectrum from cassettes and CD players to the more expensive MP3 minidisc players (around $200). There are designs of players for even very young children with large, easy-to-operate buttons, and a terrific series of cassettes that have a "read along" feature. The story is recorded with a tone to indicate when it is time to turn the page. The first couple of sentences on the page explains this to the listener and demonstrates the tone before the narrator begins the story. Preschoolers are often delighted that they can "read" without an adult. For older readers, the publishing industry has audiobooks figured out and now offers a much larger selection in both abridged and unabridged versions. If you haven't visited an audio section in a bookstore lately, check it out. The prices are a bit high ($24 and up), but used bookstores, Internet sites, and thrift stores are good sources for discounted sets. Additionally, many public libraries have significantly expanded the number of audiobooks they carry and some video stores carry audio rentals. The Cracker Barrel chain of restaurants has a program where you can rent an audiotape for a few dollars and drop the tape off at any other Cracker Barrel restaurant.

Flying With Children

Flying with children can be an adventure, but there are special considerations. If you've never flown with a child, I suggest that you recall all the things you thought about when you shared airplane space with an unruly youngster or crying baby. Flying is a new experience for a child, and there are many restrictions (sitting properly buckled into a seat while waiting on the runway immediately comes to mind) that can't be avoided. Some of the fundamentals, however, are to understand that the noise, change in altitude, drier air within the cabin, and restriction of physical space are factors that will affect your child's behavior. Children are highly susceptible to the change in altitude, and the wails that accompany take-offs and landings are frequently in response to ear pain. Sucking a bottle or pacifier usually works for an infant, and chewing gum or something like pretzel pieces works at an older age. Congestion and headaches can result from the drier air, but a preflight dose of an over-the-counter medication and extra fluids can prevent or minimize those problems.

Most airlines allow a child under the age of two to fly for no cost on a parent's lap, but if it is a long flight, consider purchasing the extra seat for your own comfort. Airlines do not normally have child safety seats available, but there are several types easily found in department stores and the right type can also serve as an automobile safety seat when you arrive at your destination. I strongly recommend a sufficient quantity of snacks and entertainment devices (with the earphones of course). Most of the entertainment systems are approved for in-flight use and must only be turned off for take-off and landing.

The additional airport security measures that have been put into place have undeniably complicated travel and commonly result in delays, flight diversions, and a definite decline in the level of courtesy and patience in many cases. I sincerely hope that the entire industry finds a way to regain its equilibrium, but until that happens, you have to be prepared that the antics of a cranky child may be enough to send other passengers and flight attendants into short-tempered, less-than-kind responses. That won't help the situation or your grated nerves, yet recognizing the potential for this unpleasantness might make it a little easier to cope with if you encounter it during your travels.

Unaccompanied Children and Flying

Our son, Dustin, took his first flight at twelve months, and, due to our family situation, he flew routinely two to three times a year after that. He was familiar with the process and viewed it as perfectly normal to have breakfast at the airport in Shreveport, Louisiana, and dinner in Damariscotta, Maine. His first unaccompanied flight at age five was a short, forty-five minute hop from Dallas, Texas, to Shreveport. I was allowed to go on board to get him settled, and, as I made sure he had his read-along books and cassette player, he kissed me good-bye with no visible sign of concern. When the woman across the aisle realized I was about to depart the airplane, she politely asked if I was going to really allow him to fly alone. She did an admirable job of erasing most of the disapproval from her face, and my father later told me that after the flight attendant escorted Dustin off the plane, "Everything was fine, and a real nice lady came up to us and said she had been watching him, and he seemed to have enjoyed the flight without being scared." Hmmm, wonder who that would have been?

At age eight, Dustin considered himself to be an accomplished traveler, and not long before his eleventh birthday, he was comfortable with the idea when circumstances caused us to book him on an unaccompanied transatlantic trip from Atlanta, Georgia, to London, England. The next solo trip was only six months later from Zurich, Switzerland, to Portland, Maine, and, by that time, he would breezily brush aside any discussion about how most preteens did not visit their grandparents in this manner.

The decision to allow a child to fly unaccompanied should come with careful thought, but it need not be a traumatic event. The checklist, "Flying A Minor Unaccompanied," lists the important points.

Some of the airlines have altered their policies since September 2001, so be sure to check with the individual airlines for specifics. For the major U.S. carriers only, the following general rules apply:

Children, five through seven, may travel unaccompanied, but cannot be on standby and cannot change planes. A parent or guardian must be with them until they are on the plane, and that adult must provide the name, address, and phone number (preferably both work and home) of the parent or guardian who will be waiting at the end of the line. A picture identification and signature of the receiving adult will be required.

Children, eight through fifteen, may have connecting flights, even with another airline, and will be escorted by airline employees. Children will not be routinely booked on late-evening flights if a connection is required. The reason for this is to minimize the possibility of having to book a child into a hotel if there is a delay, and the connecting flight is missed. Special meals can be ordered, but most airlines will not permit their personnel to administer medication to a minor. The child must be able to self-medicate.

Unaccompanied children are under the supervision of airline employees at all times, and the airline employee usually maintains the travel documents. Some airlines assign a specific flight attendant for on-board supervision; most affix distinctive badges to the children; and some have attended child care centers for layovers or unexpected delays. While sixteen is the standard age for flying independently, some airlines use age twelve as the cutoff.

There are additional costs applied as a service fee that ranges from $40 to $100, and airlines frequently do not offer discount fares to unaccompanied minors.

The rules for international travel have slight variations—children five to seven, for example, may not have stopovers in any country other than their final destination.

I have three final notes on this subject. First, try and schedule unaccompanied children on early flights whenever possible because if there are delays, the airline will have a better chance of getting the child to the destination on the same day. This is especially true if the destination is one serviced by limited carriers and/or flights.

Second, if the child is old enough, make sure she has either a portable telephone or a telephone card of some type and knows how to use it. Even though the airline will take care of any problems en route, the child very well might want to just call and have a familiar person to talk to if things are not going according to plan.

Third, the airline definition of independent at age sixteen (or younger) is fine from a flying perspective, but it can work against you in circumstances when a schedule is thrown into turmoil due to weather or some other type of significant disruption. For example, the Christmas when Dustin was fifteen, he was returning to Hawaii from Maine, and the connecting flight was grounded in Atlanta. The airline was putting everyone up in a hotel, and since he was a minor, the airline contacted my husband, who thanked them and called his parents who lived an hour away. Despite Dustin's assurances that he would have been fine on his own, they were delighted with the unexpected visit.

Had Dustin been seventeen, however, we would not have received the call, and he would have, indeed, been on his own in Atlanta. And then there is the fact that some airlines have a less-than-stellar reputation for taking care of stranded travelers. This is not a situation that you will necessarily encounter, but it's a good idea to mentally work through the process of how you would handle such an event. There have been cases where travelers have been booked on next-day flights, and no overnight lodging allowed, due to airline interpretation of their responsibility for the customers' welfare. An experienced traveler could probably get a reversal of that ruling; it would be more difficult for a tired eighteen-year-old to do so. We made arrangements with one of our credit card companies to have a separate card issued in Dustin's name when he was thirteen, even though it was actually my card. That way, he could use the card with no difficulty if he ran into travel situations that required unexpected purchases.

CHAPTER NINE

The Tables Are Turned

Oh My, They're All Gone!

I have included this chapter for two reasons, and no, my cousin had nothing to do with it. The first is because, as with some of my contemporaries, I am currently experiencing the transition of having a child head off to college, and there are some peculiar sensations connected to being the parent who is at home while the fledgling adult is away.

The second reason is because there are times when you move from stage to stage with your children that you feel like it will never end. A few years ago, one of our neighbors, whose husband was in the Navy and frequently on travel, was juggling a two-and-a-half year old son and a newborn daughter. She had put her external career on hold, and while she was certain that was the right choice for her, there were moments when she was almost convinced that her brain would no longer be able to grasp anything beyond the realm of Walt Disney characters. I was always a working/traveling mother, although on the weekends when my son was young, I would sometimes have the same thoughts. But when you sit through your child's high school graduation, you suddenly wonder where those years went.

Several friends asked me if I thought I was ready for the change after our son had been accepted into the University of Maine. I told them that with all the separations we'd been through as a family, I probably wouldn't really notice until he'd been gone for at least a month. That was a slight exaggeration, and I have to say that it was an adjustment to see his empty room and remember when I went grocery shopping that we wouldn't need a box of macaroni and cheese or frozen chicken tenders until Christmas time.

Although we have only our son, the parents I have spoken to who have more than one child acknowledge that the feelings of separation can be just as palpable the second or third time around. And yes, the emotional spectrum is rather lengthy with several sets of parents who have smilingly declared that the empty nest has become the best part of their lives and that they're like the couple in the television advertisement that can hardly wait for their daughter to clear the driveway before they start packing to go off on a vacation.

I met Mary, a delightful lady, not long after her only son entered college, and he stayed in place when they were reassigned to a new area. Mary and her son had often coped with her husband's extended absences, and she was surprised to find that she actually missed her son's company more than she had her husband's.

"I don't know," she said one time. "I guess that I was so used to the tradition of being the good military wife and being supportive of my soldier husband being gone that I didn't realize how empty it would seem when it was our son instead. I just wasn't prepared for how intense the feeling is. Having your child gone is different, even though I know he's an adult, or at least I keep telling myself that he is."

Mary embraced e-mail with great enthusiasm, and when I last spoke with her, she had become more comfortable with her empty nest and wasn't even anxious to start filling it back up with visiting grandchildren.

Debbie, another friend of mine who had spent several years as a single parent, related her rueful recollection of her daughter's departure. "I put a lot of effort into teaching her to be independent and how to cope with the times that I was gone. After she left to be on her own I had to remind myself that this meant she'd learned exactly what I wanted her to."

Debbie wasn't one to spend too long in maudlin thought, and in relatively short order she shrugged off the reminiscenses and had her daughter's bedroom converted into a great home office—although she did buy a new sleeper sofa for the den.

Another woman that I recently met at a party smiled when I was talking about the different reactions, and she said that quite honestly, she and her husband had to reevaluate their own relationship after the children were gone. They had been caught up in the hectic lifestyle that many parents encounter with multiple children in an activity-laden environment. The suddenly quiet house, combined with the realization that they finally had evenings and weekends free, meant they had to decide whether it was time they wanted to spend doing things together or independently pursuing their own hobbies and interests. She said that between that and learning how to cook again for only two people, it was a transition that had taken more thought than she had anticipated.

A comprehensive book *Fighting for Your Empty Nest Marriage* (2000), by a group of five authors, covers virtually every aspect of empty nesting. David H. Arp, Claudia S. Arp, Scott M. Stanley, Howard J. Markman, and Susan Blumberg conducted a tremendous amount of research to buttress a serious discussion of the kinds of issues that marriages can encounter as the children depart the day-to-day scene.

Oh My, I Thought They Were Gone!

Then, of course, there are those families where the initial excursion out of the nest doesn't last, usually due either to an unexpected downturn in post-high school education plans or to economic crunches—especially in high cost of living areas.

Lawrence Kutner mentions this in another section of his book *Making Sense of Your Teenager.* His research showed that "the proportion of young adults who are supported by their parents reached a thirty year high in the mid 1980s. . . . According to the 1984 Census Bureau figures, 53 percent of men and 32 percent of women between the ages of twenty and twenty-four were living with or having their expenses paid by their parents. This had increased from 40 percent and 26 percent, respectively, a decade earlier."[1]

More recent figures show the percentage of males has dropped to 33 percent, although the age span has increased to up to thirty-four years old.

It should come as no surprise that the primary reason adult children move back home is financial. There are several different basic scenarios and an almost endless number of variations on those scenarios, but if an adult child returns home, perhaps the most important question is: How long is this for? Next is, How much should I/we intervene? All kinds of personal factors come into play in these situations, and I'll just use three examples that I am familiar with.

Example One is the newly graduated high school or college student who was absolutely, positively certain that she was ready to move out. She had even done the math correctly and worked through the kind of money she needed, found an appropriate place to live, and had enough furnishings, dishes, and so forth to survive. If a roommate is required to succeed, that's one of the first things that can go awry. The roommate either isn't a good match, falls in love and moves out or wants to move a significant other in, etc. If a roommate is not involved or is not a problem, then, maybe, the job falls through or the transportation arrangements come unraveled, or the unexpected expenses mount too rapidly. ("Well, gosh, I never realized car insurance and utilities cost so much.")

Instances like this are usually short-term and, many times, parents are prepared for this early setback having either been through it themselves or having been skeptical of the job/roommate/living accommodations, or whatever, in the first place. And while you may feel that an "I-told-you-so/Tried-to-tell-you" is in order, the satisfaction gained from expressing the sentiment may not be terribly productive.

The loss of a job can be particularly traumatic and, depending on the local employment environment, may be fairly easy to overcome or may prove difficult. The key, as with other aspects of parenting, is to be supportive without being crippling. The fact that the initial foray into the "real" world wasn't permanent doesn't mean that the return home will be lengthy. It is important to determine the root problem in order to work through a solution and, in all likelihood, parental advice that might have been spurned when planning the initial move-out will probably be considered valuable at this point.

Example Two tends to be far more disquieting and usually involves separation or divorce, perhaps complete with small child or children in tow. Duration and required intervention in these situations can be tricky since volatile emotions and legal tugs-of-war are almost inevitably part of the mix. Interestingly, this particular return to the nest can also segue into parent-child, work-related separation due to the need or desire to put geographical distance between the estranged former spouses and the complications of trying to handle relocation in a single-parent status. There is, however, ordinarily, an incentive to regain independent living space as quickly as possible, although financial stability can be elusive if the adult child had no means of support outside the marriage. I'm not going to spend any more time in this area precisely because it often requires qualified legal or certified counseling assistance or both.

Example Three is the one that is relatively new from a sociological perspective. That is the one of the adult child who returns home because they either cannot "find" themselves or cannot achieve the lifestyle level to which they were accustomed when growing up. That is not to say it is inadvisable to provide your children with a spacious home and whatever amenities you can afford. I simply want to mention that if you have a reached the stage of a large home, nice cars, resort vacations with the family, and frequent dining at nice restaurants, it can come as an unpleasant surprise for a young adult that most entry level jobs will not enable her or him to have that same degree of comfort.

Notwithstanding the second sample scenario, how can you help ensure the departure of the adult child is effective? While the old joke of moving and leaving no forwarding address can work, I personally recommend there be some guidelines candidly discussed in the late teen years. Is college expected? If so, is it just undergraduate, or beyond? If you and the child have aspirations for graduate or professional school, the ability to do that and earn enough money to live independently may be mutually exclusive.

Do you live in a high-cost area where there is a shortage of available affordable housing? If so, that's something that has to be planned for. Has your child received any life-skill preparation? It's a part of many middle- and high-school curricula, but is by no means standard teaching. If a teenager has never worked at a paying job, doesn't understand the difference between earnings and take-home pay, and has no genuine idea of what it costs to maintain a household, it is easy to become overwhelmed with the kind of trade-offs that must often be made when starting out.

The management of consumer debt is perhaps one of the best indicators of whether or not an adult child will need to seek refuge back at home. The startling increase in young adult debt has been a topic of recent discussion, and many of the same characteristics that result in burdensome debt can cause a young adult to feel unable to cope with life outside the safety net of parental income. There are many articles to consult, and the book, *Debt Proof Your Kids* by Mary Hunt, is an excellent source if you want to get into some detail. Her recommendations provide a plan that begins in the elementary school years. If you're either already past that point, or feel that's a bit young to start, there are still numerous useful techniques that can help build a solid understanding of financial reality in what is a tempting world of easy credit and quicksand debt. I don't want to diverge too far from the primary topic of this book, but if you think financial independence for your children is a given with no preparation, you should probably rethink that assumption.

For nearly four years, one of my coworkers fit right into the category of parenting that extended well beyond when she had anticipated. She joked that they should have installed a revolving door and lamented that she would never be without grown children at home. The last of their three children did eventually find gainful employment along with an affordable apartment. She laughed about it afterwards and said it was the first time she'd noticed how large the house was and how little of it she and her husband used by themselves. I'm pretty certain that she expects to have grandchildren filling the unoccupied space before too much longer, and she's been talking about starting the long-postponed kitchen remodeling project.

Even if you're not close to the time, you might want to sit down at some point and read over the checklist, "The Empty Nest As A Place To *Visit*." The key elements to consider are provided, and you may have unique family factors to add that will tailor the list for your own situation.

There are also circumstances that draw adult children home from a practical perspective. Some homes are designed with multifamily living in mind, and perhaps the health of one or both parents becomes a factor. A family-run business, where living and working are in close proximity, is another reason for extended family arrangements—arrangements that can be temporary or otherwise. In these cases, the desire for empty-nesting might have never existed, or it might simply be mutually agreed that it is not an issue of concern.

And lastly, there are empty-nest situations when the adjustment doesn't go smoothly at all. The cognitive acceptance of letting go may, or may not, actually prepare you for the day when it happens. For some parents, the departure of the child (oops, young adult) is easier to cope with than the idea that they are now at the stage of their lives to *have* an offspring old enough to leave the nest. A very dear friend had more or less gracefully accepted becoming middle-aged and prepared herself for this new point. She had become involved in an investment club and a book group, as two new interests, and was pleased with her foresight. Her justifiable satisfaction was shattered when she discovered that her husband had chosen instead to plunge into a messy and irrevocable mid-life crisis complete with a younger woman. That, however, is another story.

CHAPTER TEN

Stories From Around

I've taken the other stories and comments that were sent to me and arrayed them here in a topical manner. As it turned out, I did not receive input from children, although there are some interesting insights from young adults and college students. There is a mix of ages, gender, and occupations. This input is more heavily weighted toward emotional response and personal philosophy on the overall impact of family separation than it is on practical tips. For some, it is the affirmation of feelings, and for others, it seemed to be an opportunity to voice a sentiment that might have otherwise gone unexpressed. It is not, however, an across-the-board sweep of cheery anecdotes. There are flashes of anger and resentment of the sort that can realistically be expected when families are faced with the issue of separation. And despite my personal belief in the ability to positively manage this aspect of our lives, I think it is extremely important to remember that, at times, the sacrifices asked of a family may be too high a price to be paid.

Fortunately, I did not receive anything that was not printable in a publication of this nature. Therefore, the only changes that I made to any of the entries was to correct some spelling. I have used some of the input as direct quotes, and others I have paraphrased.

I do hope that the people who chose not to be identified check back on my site (charliehudson.net) periodically so they know when the book is released and have a chance to see that what they wrote or e-mailed was included.

CAREER WOMEN ON THE ROAD

Two of my friends who wrote in both became mothers after they were firmly established in their careers; one is military and the other is a Department of the Army civilian.

Marcia Enyart, a retired Lieutenant Colonel in Northern Virginia, took very little time between retirement from the Army and entering motherhood. It was a bit of a surprise to some of us, but she assured us she was ready for the challenge. After the momentous occasion, she also went to work for a large, well-known firm, although she was able to hold off travel until her daughter was five months old. Between her and her husband, they averaged two to four trips per year, usually for no more than a week at a time. As Marcia explained:

> Getting ready to go was the worst. Once I was on my way and busy with my work, I was much better. Knowing that my daughter was safe and well taken care of with my husband and my father, and realizing that my real fear is that she wouldn't miss me was important. It was reassuring to know that she noticed my absence—the day care providers commented on it, but it was more reassuring to know that she was in good care with my husband and could survive without my "presence."

Janet Truesdale, the Army civilian, married to a gentleman who retired from the government civil service, took a position that was originally supposed to be short-duration projects. Not surprisingly, that arrangement very rapidly moved into not only continual work, but also frequent travel. Janet and Ron soon found themselves to be one of the couples who have to try and de-conflict their travel schedules, so they can meet the commitments of both jobs and their two young children. Fortunately, Janet's parents can usually help out when sudden changes in either schedule can have them in a bind. There have been several occasions when Janet and I would be at meetings together, and she would be virtually breathless from the hectic pace. Janet finally had a moment to send me an e-mail:

> Our daughter was only about six months of age when I had to start traveling, and it seems like our son was younger than that. With both of us in the kinds of jobs we have, it probably averages about one week per month that we are absent. Calling on the phone in the morning and the evening and having the grandparents actively involved are the most effective tools I find for coping with it.

WIVES WHO WAIT

Eileen Ledbetter has been an Army wife for more than twenty years and, until this most recent assignment, her husband served in units that frequently deployed for training, often on short notice. His current job is more stable, the children are older now, and Eileen's job requires minimal travel. She recalled the earlier years, however, when she had to quickly learn the unwritten rules about Army life. Eileen wrote an excellent article published in the Army Times in 2001. It was in response to a study entitled *Invisible Women* that had set off a controversy, due to certain characteristics that the author of the study had attributed to the young wives of enlisted personnel. Eileen's perceptive article touched on a number of relative points, and she stressed the need to develop strong coping skills as well as an understanding of military life.[1] She was a natural source for me to talk to about this book, and she gave some solid tips for families during the separation piece:

> There were several-week-long to a month separations when the children were small, but Desert Storm had the biggest impact. Our children were seven, five, and eighteen months at the time. Now that the children are older, we seem to have fewer separations. When they were young, separations averaged around two or three month-long absences a year.
>
> The most effective way to cope with separation is to have a plan. Whenever my husband was away for more than a week or two I would have a goal (clean the linen closet . . .) and give myself time to do it without having to rush. Also, I would spend a lot of time with the kids, just being silly. This helped them to deal with the separation too. We'd draw pictures and write letters to daddy. There were lots of nights we'd camp out in the living room and eat junk food! It was fun. The children also were more inclined to help out around the house and cooperate if I made things fun.
>
> I don't really have one particular story that sticks out in my mind to share with people, but it seemed like every time my husband went away, something major would happen. Someone would break a bone or run a fever. I can't count the number of times my car was hit while he was away—he started to think it was me—it wasn't! I swear—They hit me! My only real advice for someone dealing with a separation is to keep a sense of humor about things—it'll be over before you know it!"

Brenda Elliott, another experienced Army wife, braced herself for the year that her husband, Paul, was assigned to Korea in the pre-e-mail days. Their three daughters were stair-stepped, with Erica as the oldest. She told me that she found it the most helpful to keep photographs of family activities around, especially in the girls' bedroom. That way she was able to use them to let Erica talk about fun things they did together, and for Alicia to keep her father's image in mind. The baby, Andrea, was too young to understand, but even the telephone calls at least provided the sound of Paul's voice. Letters and drawings were something the girls could do and that was something they enjoyed.

Carrie Gissiner, the woman who runs the Sergeant Mom's website discussed in Part Two, had this to share:

I've been a Navy wife for almost 19 years now—officially 19 on Aug 13th! We have a 16-year-old son and a 13-year-old daughter. (Yes, we've hit the really fun stage!) We've done shore duty (Wing-11, VP-30), aircraft carriers (USS Forrestal and USS America) and a P-3 squadron (VP-45) for sea duty. The worst stretch to not see my husband was in a 16-month period: we saw him a total of 93 days. Of course it was all hit and miss, a few days here, a week there, etc. Right now, he is on shore duty for the first time in more than 10 years, and this is the longest period he has been home! For the past 14 months, with the exception of one week, he has been home. I keep telling myself this is practice for retirement! Actually, he will not be hitting retirement for another 5–6 years. He did 4 years active duty, then went into the Reserves for about 4–5 years, and then came back to active duty. So, we have 4–5 years before retirement, unless they raise the amount of time he can stay. Right now he can stay for 22 years, and he plans on staying in until they kick him out. (He doesn't know what he want to do when he grows up!) He truly enjoys the flying and doesn't want to give it up.

WHEN IT IS UNEXPECTED

Kim, a Pennsylvanian and member of the Army Reserve, was so excited when she was finally able to transfer from the post office where she worked to one close to her house. It was a wonderful setup, and she had time in the morning to help get her son off to school, fix breakfast for her daughter, and her commute had been reduced to about fifteen minutes. The enjoyment lasted for only a short while when she was activated for a year in support of Operations Noble Eagle and Enduring Freedom. The good news was that she would be working in an operations center in Alexandria, Virginia, rather than deploying overseas. The other fortunate aspect of the mobilization was that she would be able to stay with her sister near Alexandria. She tried to remember those two good points as she and her husband made the painful decision for their six-year-old son to remain with him in Pennsylvania, while she and their daughter made the move. They were grateful that they would be able to have at least a weekend marriage, even though it was not something they expected to happen. As Kim said,

"Telephone calls and weekend visits were important, but I feel like there is a void in my life with my family separated. The best advice that I can offer is to just keep in touch with your loved ones and the time will pass a lot easier."

Beth, from North Carolina, sent an interesting observation about one summer when she and her husband were in the Air Force and Army Reserves, respectively. The first time they both had to be away at the same time was when their son was five. It was for a couple of months, but the situation was such that he was able to stay with his father's parents during the entire length of the separation.

Coping with the separation turned out to be fairly noneventful, yet when Beth returned home shortly before her husband, and went to her in-laws to spend a few days and retrieve their son, she was startled to discover some changes that she hadn't thought about.

He had been through one of those growth spurts as young children do, was able to show off cartwheels, and had started eating foods he'd never cared for before. Beth was a bit chagrined to admit that she had more or less expected the time she was gone to be "frozen," and it simply hadn't occurred to her that their son would be the least bit different than he was the day they had dropped him off.

An unsigned contribution was another one of the e-mails I received that brought back some of the painful memories of being away.

I don't want to tell you my name because I know I wasn't the only person this happened to, and I don't want my family to think that I am complaining. My sister and her husband were both in the Army, and I had

agreed to be the temporary guardian if they needed me to. I didn't actually expect to have to, but they were sent to the Gulf during the war. It
isn't that I minded, but their son was three, and their daughter was only
five months old. I couldn't believe the Army would take both parents away
like that. My brother-in-law left two weeks before she did, and she flew
home to bring the kids to our place. My sister was really upset even
though she tried to act like it was all right to the kids. We took her to the
airport and made up big banners and everything, but when she kissed my
nephew good-bye and then handed me the baby, it was all I could do not
to burst into tears. It was just one of the saddest things I'd ever seen.

The woman went on to describe the almost seven months that
passed with erratic communications due to the mail, her concern
with attempting to explain the absence to her nephew, her concern
that her niece wouldn't know who her parents were, and her ever-
present fear that one or both parents would be harmed.

Their two sons were ages four and six, so that helped tremen-
dously with the three-year-old, and her sister had made some family
videotapes that the child watched. The aunt also showed photographs of her sister and brother-in-law to her infant niece and spoke
about "Mommy and Daddy," even though she had no idea if that
would help her niece connect the words to the faces. More than anything, she tried to protect the children from grim media predictions
of protracted, bloody battles. She said that she wanted to forbid the
boys from playing soldier, but her husband stepped in and said that
was going too far, and, apparently, he took care to spend time with
them talking about how important and patriotic it was for soldiers to
defend the country.

The parents did return with no difficulty, and to great celebration
to include a daughter who was now walking, talking, and, yes, who
soon correctly identified "Mommy and Daddy" with no problem.
This did turn out to be the only time the sister had to step in as a
guardian, although she felt that the military policy of sending both
parents away should be changed. She also observed that the extended absence did not seem to have a lasting effect on the children.

I'm going to insert an author's note here and mention once again
that it truly does make a difference when children are assured that a
parent, or parents', absence serves a purpose. This is something that

can be discussed with even very young children as long as you can find something they can relate to. In a case like the one described above, I wouldn't recommend geopolitical lessons, but I'm willing to bet the three-year-old was familiar with "heroes" and "villains" or "someone taking something that didn't belong to him" so that his mother and father "were helping make it right," if you prefer terms a bit less judgmental.

A SINGLE MOM'S DISCOVERY

One woman wrote in with an experience that was unlike anything that I had ever been through, but I suspect that she is correct is thinking that other single parents might be in a similar situation.

She divorced out of an abusive marriage, despite a significant decline in financial support and two young daughters to care for. She was able to depend on her parents for emotional, if not monetary, help and to work out of her apartment and to eventually move into a home with her home-based business. It was a struggle to reestablish herself, and her interests were centered around creating a safe and stable environment for her family. She had no real social life beyond their tight circle, and this was the pattern for more than two years.

Circumstances dictated that she needed to attend an important business conference several states away, and she was extremely reluctant to make the trip and leave her daughters alone. Her parents, and her mother in particular, insisted that there was nothing to worry about and that she should take the opportunity to go and mingle with other people in her line of work.

She was nervous and hesitant and ultimately relieved to learn that their advice had been sound. Everything ran smoothly at home, the girls' didn't seem to feel abandoned, and she met other women that she could network with. It was an enlightening time for her, and she realized that she had, in truth, isolated herself more than was probably necessary for the well-being of her family. After the trip, she was able to become involved in a number of activities beyond the home circle that she had created.

The last part of her message summed up her main point:

> We all still spend a lot of time together, and working at home lets me be
> very flexible with my hours, and I don't usually take more than one or two

trips a year without them, but if my mother hadn't convinced me to go on that first trip, I don't know when I might have changed my mind. I think all single parents have to be very careful about balancing work and children, but leaving them sometimes isn't automatically a bad idea. It doesn't mean you aren't doing your job as a parent.

MIXED EMOTIONS

It's easy for children (not to mention spouses) to feel conflicted about the issue of travel. I'm not sure how old the person was who sent this, nor did he provide a name. (I assume it was a *he*, but maybe I'm being sexist.)

> You know, it bothered me for a long time that my dad was never around to see me play baseball. He traveled a lot and especially in the spring. I was good, too, and hardly ever spent any time on the bench, but my dad wasn't one of the ones in the bleachers. My mom worked too, but she wasn't much into sports, and she did come to some of the games even though I knew she didn't really understand what the game was about. My dad would ask me about the games and brag about me around folks, but it's not like he got to see for himself. Then I finally decided that I really liked to play ball and what were my choices—stop playing because he wasn't there? And I don't know, maybe if I had told him it would have made a difference, but I don't think so. And he was a great guy mostly. It's kind of funny. I suppose that I didn't mind him being gone most of the time. It just would have been really nice if he could have been around for baseball season.

Another e-mail came in from a young man who only identified himself as John.

His feelings were strong in the sense that he had genuinely resented his father's constant absences even though he never allowed his resentment to be projected in destructive ways. He kept his grades up, didn't confront his parents, and didn't get into trouble to attract their attention.

His understanding of the demands of the military on his father was tempered by a belief that not all the intensive assignments that his father took were really necessary. His father's inability to attend his high school graduation was something that still bothered him deeply.

His own plans for his future included a vision of some kind of profession that enabled him to have greater control over his time to be able to spend it with the family he hoped to have someday.

Keri, from Knoxville, Tennessee, sent a long e-mail that spoke of an interesting observation.

Her dual-career parents traveled on business from her earliest memories.

The ability of her grandparents to help out kept the adult coverage in her life inside the family, and the airline miles accumulated primarily by her father enabled them to take semi-annual vacations to exotics places like the Bahamas and Singapore.

She also felt that the willingness of her parents to allow her to function independently for short periods when she was in high school contributed to her being better prepared for college life.

Their frequent habit of "family time" being spent in various airports didn't particularly bother her, but she was disconcerted when she overheard them argue about domestic matters and exchange barbs about each caring more about work than family. Those kinds of arguments made her wonder if some of the travel was a means to avoid dealing with other emotional issues.

It wasn't a topic that she chose to discuss with her parents, and she closed her e-mail with the comment that she was doing well in college and "they were still together, so I guessed everything was all right."

WHEN THE HUSBAND IS AT HOME

There are, no doubt, families where the household and parenting duties are so equally divided that either parent can travel and the other slides right in and manages with no difficulty. And in all fairness, I do know at least half a dozen men, to include my husband, who have done duty as the stay-at-home parent and accomplished the tasks with no lasting ill effect. One of the interesting aspects when you start a project like this, however, is the different perspectives you encounter when dealing with similar scenarios.

Two men, Dan and Harry, each did what was for them a role reversal with their wives one summer when they stayed at home with the children and managed the house; in one case, it was while the wife attended a two-week conference, and the other situation was a month for a training class of some kind.

There were two children in Dan's family and three in Harry's, but the age range was almost identical and both men were hard-charging, military guys who could hold their own on a basketball court and had no shortage when it came to testosterone levels.

Dan looked back on it as a humbling experience that he was in no hurry to repeat. It is not that he didn't love his wife and appreciate his children; he simply had never been faced with the myriad details required to keep a household from descending into chaos. Nor was he prepared to explain why it was Mommy gone this time instead of him. After all, *he* was the one who routinely packed his flight bag, kissed everyone good-bye, and eventually reappeared to a welcoming family.

"God, I had no idea it was so tough," he told me with a grin. "Liz had fixed some meals and put them in the freezer, had things organized, and left instructions about where the kids were supposed to be when, but it was like there were these constant questions. And always, 'Mommy doesn't do it that way.' I mean, hell, what difference does it make if I cut the crusts off the sandwich or not? After two days, I was unbelievably grateful when one of the neighbors came over just to see how things were and stayed for a cup of coffee. It was the first adult conversation I'd had except for when Liz called. Not that it changed the amount of time that I had to be away after that, but I was a whole lot more sympathetic, and I got a whole lot better about keeping in touch when I was deployed. I just had never realized that it really mattered."

Harry was more nonchalant and shrugged good-naturedly. "It's not that big a deal if you plan things out," he said when the subject came up at work one day. "You don't try and mess with the routine, and you pay attention to what goes on before the wife leaves. Sure, I know guys who don't have a clue where the laundry detergent is, and they'd just as soon live off pizza and chocolate ice cream to keep the kids happy. We bumped heads a few times over some stuff and sure, I got the 'I wish Mom was here—she'd know what to do,' a couple of times, but we worked it all out. Teresa [his wife] quizzed me kind of hard that first few phone calls, but she was enjoying the course she was taking, she was with a group of people she liked, and it was a nice break for her. It didn't take her too long to relax, even though I think towards the end of the month, she was ready to come home. It wasn't a complete walk in the park for us, but we all came out of it just fine."

SOMETIMES HOME, USUALLY GONE

"Look," a friend of mine said, "Guys aren't going to sit around and talk about their feelings, but if you promise not to use my name, then okay, I'll tell you what I worry about when I'm not home for months at a time. It bothers me that I can't be there to play catch with my son. I mean, my wife probably won't think to offer to do that, and if my son gets her to, well, you know, no offense, but she throws like a girl. It bothers me when something breaks around the house, and I know my wife will have to deal with that while she's working and doing other things. And she'll have to call someone in because she's not the handyman type. It's not that I mind the cost, but I actually like to do that sort of stuff, and I know for sure that I'll do it right. It bothers me that I had to miss the Pinewood Derby. [Annual Cub Scout event. The boys make cars from a block of wood and then have races—gravity powered, not motorized]. I was able to help my son get the car built when I was home for a weekend, but I couldn't be there to help him put on the finishing touches or the night of the Derby. My wife meant well, but she didn't know about the little adjustments that you can make or putting graphite on the wheels. Our son came in dead last, and he tried to sound okay about it, but I know he was disappointed. The worst part was that I know it would have been better if I had been there. Okay, the world didn't fall apart, but it's the kind of things fathers and sons do together."

My friend continued his explanation with concerns about how he was supposed to manage when he was home and his wife wasn't. He was up-front about not knowing how to care for a sick child and acknowledged that he felt the real root for many couples was the issue of different skill sets. He was adverse to involved emotional discussions, but he did feel that couples needed to work out how the multiple aspects of parenting would be handled when either one was required to fill the role of both. Of course, what he actually wanted was a way to get the information he needed without getting into the "touchy-feely" business.

I'm not sure there are enough checklists to allow for that, but I do agree with him that if both parents know they will be swapping roles on a regular basis, they should think about any gender-related impact on the children. For example, if a daughter is approaching the age when that first brassiere needs to be purchased, and, for some reason, mom won't be available, the help of another female relative or friend can be enlisted. In this example, the parents can also go together to a lingerie shop or department so he can either get some idea of what he will be facing or arrange to have sales assistance if the shopping trip is required.

A GRANDFATHER CHECKING IN

This letter was especially interesting in view of the military background. It was from Dennis in Virginia.

My wife saw your note in a newsletter and insisted that I write you about a decision we made after I retired from more than thirty years in the Army. Like all military families, we had somewhere around twenty moves during my career, and I was deployed often for varying lengths of time at each of those locations. Despite the fact that my wife wasn't truly aware of what life would be like as an Army wife, she took it all in stride and raised our three children with me hop-scotching around the globe. She was certainly the *Wind Beneath My Wings* and instilled a strong sense in our children that they shouldn't resent my absences.

Our oldest son followed in my footsteps, but our other son and daughter chose to settle here in the Northern Virginia area. We knew we would be returning here after I retired and as my wife and I were weighing the different job offers that I had received, I was naturally leaning towards one that was extremely lucrative. The more I looked at the extensive global travel requirements, the more I thought about the years that I had lost with my children and my wife. There's no way I could count the birthdays and other special events that I had missed. My wife and I talked it over and as always, she was willing to support me no matter which job I chose.

I chose a comfortable, but lower salary position with practically no travel involved. Our son and daughter that are here have spouses who also work and we have become their safety net for taking care of the kids when they have to be on the road. My wife and I are both in wonderful health and this arrangement has worked out quite well for everyone so far. In addition to work trips, we have filled in so the adult kids can go off occasionally for a romantic weekend.

I don't regret the time in the Army for a single moment; it's something that I am proud of, but this has been a good way to balance out what I wasn't able to do for our children when they were younger.

WHEN THERE ISN'T A BALANCE

As I mentioned at the beginning of this chapter, not everyone views separation with the same philosophy. Tonya from Delaware began having to cope with routine separations when their son was only six months old. She focuses on "staying physically fit . . . working out . . . shopping . . . anything to make the day go by faster." Yet even with that, it is always a struggle:

> Every time my husband leaves, my son and I have a clash. He is six, and my husband is away right now. I am aggravated being an only parent, and my son is aggravated being once again without his daddy. So after two weeks (almost always it is the two-week mark) we come to a "head," and I have to spank him. He is disrespectful and disobedient after his dad leaves. I try to deal with it in an understanding way, but that accomplishes nothing. Once I put my foot down and reestablish my authority, my authority ALONE, he starts obeying. But he misses his dad, and it is evident in the dark circles under his eyes, his poor appetite, and his emotional ups and downs.
>
> People with children should not be in the military. It is selfish to think you can have a career in the military and still have children. Something has to give, and it is always the child. And at the end of twenty long years, you look back and see the ALL you gave the military at the expense of your kid, and once you retire, the military doesn't even remember your name.
>
> How many "successful" military officers (colonels and above) are still married to the wife of their youth? I've attended many promotions. Almost without exception, when the promotee refers to his children helping make it all possible, the children look at the floor. And the wife, well, the children's mother usually isn't there.
>
> Being a good leader and a good parent in today's military is an oxymoron.

Another woman echoed similar feelings, although from a corporate perspective.

A girl I play bridge with was talking about having sent something to you, and I thought that maybe you needed a dose of the other side of separation. I don't know if you will print anything that sounds negative, or if you just want the warm-hearted stories. At first I wasn't going to, but then I thought 'Why not?' I'm not going to give a lot of detail, but I have been the perfect corporate wife, run the perfectly decorated, well-organized house, give lovely parties, and for all intents and purposes have raised our two daughters alone. My husband has spent their entire lives making deals and solving everybody else's problems. For a long time, I actually thought he regretted being gone as often as he was and that he really meant to take a desk job as soon as he could. But that was never it. He's changed companies and never once truly tried to cut back on travel, even though he was given an opportunity and could have made just as much money with far fewer trips. It's the prestige and the pure ego of being the one who can drop anything at a moment's notice and rush off to fix a crisis or negotiate a tricky bargain or whatever. He has this reputation as a go-to guy and he loves it. For him, a trip to Washington in the morning, New York in the evening, and across the country or an ocean later that week is simply an affirmation of his value. A few years of that is one thing, but nearly three decades worth isn't because he has no other option.

The primary point of the rest of her submission was that she knew her husband provided well for them and cared about them in his own way, despite being essentially oblivious to the personalities of his family. She didn't think that their daughters had been adversely affected by his attitude, but she also understood that they didn't have a particularly close relationship with him. Her perspective was that some men (and no doubt women) were either not able, or not willing, to make family a priority over a profession. Her view was that in such cases, women shouldn't expend emotional resources or assign blame for something they couldn't change.

Reflection, humor, guilt, resentment, acceptance, understanding, and poignancy—not a bad summary for how work-related separations can affect families.

CHAPTER ELEVEN

Summing It All Up

Millions of parents face family separations and work-related travel on a regular basis, and for some, it is a no-big-deal, take-it-right-in-stride, fact of life. For others, there are emotional ups and downs as well as questions about how to best handle the situation. And as with so many aspects of family dynamics, the answers to the questions will vary: vary from person to person and time period to time period. Your family structure, the ages of your children, and the frequency of your absences are all factors that come into play.

It is important to recognize that the dynamics of family separations are likely to shift as your children enter different developmental stages or if the amount and/or duration of your travel changes.

One of the most vital points for successfully dealing with time away is solid, two-way communication that begins at the earliest ages. Good communications are of course critical in all relationships, but for parents who must travel, the ability to be away without creating the impression that the ones at home have been "left behind" is what is paramount. I hope that the tips provided in the preceding chapters are either adaptable for you in whole or, at least, will serve as a start for your own good ideas.

So, as a reminder:

- Acknowledge that separation anxiety will occur for your family and, maybe, for yourself. Be willing to discuss it, but don't dwell on it.

•Make an effort to explain your departures and homecomings in terms your children can comprehend, and don't be caught by surprise if you are temporarily treated to hostile behavior when you "disappear" and "reappear." Infants and toddlers may not have vocabulary skills, yet they are keenly aware when their routines are interrupted.

•Take the time to listen to older children if they express concern about why you are gone and involve them in some way in your travel if they are interested. Take them with you occasionally *if* it is practical. Recognize that it won't be more often than it will be.

•Do what you can to let them know you are available, even when you're not at home. Telephone, e-mail, buy a web cam, or just be willing to take extra time when you do return to discuss the things that are on their minds.

•Minimize missing those events that they consider significant, and if you must be away, take steps to be as much a part of the event as you can.

•Bringing gifts home is usually a good idea, but it's not a substitute for your time.

•Take measures to ensure that medical emergencies can be handled in your absence, and don't panic if one occurs.

•Understand that you can't be gone and in control at home at the same time—it doesn't work and it's not fair. Work through control matters at the adult level, but pay attention to what the children are saying and recognize that this will probably be more of an issue than any other factor as the children move through adolescence and the teen years.

•Periodically assess the impact of travel on your family and on you. If you reach the stage where you begin to resent or dread trips, or if your children exhibit persistent physical or emotional difficulty, then it may be time for a change.

•Be aware of, and honest about, what you want from your job. If your absences result in difficulty at home, don't automatically assume travel is the root cause.

Finally, I know that if you're a new parent or are just approaching the threshold of parenthood, it will be difficult to imagine that you'll be an empty-nester someday. I can almost promise, though, that for all those moments when time seems to be stalled, it isn't. The gurgling infant becomes a toddler; the "terrible twos" pass; the elementary years gain momentum; you do manage to survive the turbulence of adolescence, and at the end of the teenage roller coaster you have an adult—a real-life, old enough to vote/drink/be employed human being. If you had to miss portions of that time while you were gone, do your best to minimize any adverse impact—you can't get the years back.

I admit that it can be problematic when trying to assess whether or not travel is adversely impacting your family. The stories submitted for this book provided a mixture of situations for comparison, but if you prefer a Hollywood version, there were a couple of illustrative scenes from a short-lived television drama, *Gideon's Crossing,* that was centered around a big-city research hospital.

The main character, Dr. Gideon, was played by the talented Andre Braugher. In the premier episode, a wealthy and arrogant businessman, played by Bruce McGill, was diagnosed with what had been determined to be a hopeless form of cancer. Since this is not a critique of the show, I'll cut through what were some interesting scenes to say that Dr. Gideon did accept the businessman for treatment with an experimental drug regimen.

A number of medical ethics questions and other dramatic issues surfaced during the program, including the relationship the man had with his family as he had powered his way to phenomenal financial success. There was a tense conversation where his wife struck back at his sarcasm by telling him the reason his grown children hadn't come to give him emotional support was because they had learned from him that emotional support wasn't important. As the children had grown older, she had run out of plausible excuses for why their father was usually engaged in a business trip or deal instead of being at home.

In a follow-on scene toward the end of the episode, the businessman and Dr. Gideon were talking about the man's approach to life. He shrugged and said something along the lines of, "It was a game.

Everything was. Could I get you to give me an experimental treatment? Could I beat this cancer? My whole life has been that way. Could I make a better deal than the other guy? Could I get someone to agree to my terms to my advantage? How many times could I humiliate my wife and still have her willing to stay with me? How many birthdays could I miss and have my children still care?" At this point, he paused and said, "Guess I overplayed my hand on that one," and then he continued with another few sentences.

In that one pause and acknowledgement lies the kernel of the key question. Where is your family in your priorities? Having them as a top priority doesn't equal never traveling and doesn't mean you won't be separated—having them as a true priority means you will mitigate the effect of the travel as much as possible. Individuals and families have different ways to demonstrate emotion; the boisterous hugging of some is not comfortable for others who might prefer quiet words of affection or those who communicate through nonverbal exchanges of support.

Just as there is no "ideal" emotional interaction among family members, there is not a single "right" answer for parents who must be away. I sincerely believe that a variety of solutions and approaches can work. I also believe, however, that you don't want to look around one day and discover you have inadvertently taught your children that togetherness and demonstrating that you care are not important.

Talk to your spouse, your extended family, close friends, or even an expert or two if you want some outside advice, but especially talk to your children and pay genuine attention to what's going on around you. Keep the lines of communication open and ride out the bumps along the way together as a family. It doesn't matter if the family is dual parent, single parent, or joint custody, the caring is what counts—it always has, and it always will.

CHAPTER TWELVE

Handy Checklists

MEDICAL AND EMERGENCY TREATMENT INFORMATION

Note: Keep the filled-out checklist in a clearly marked folder and either put the folder in the same place as the list of emergency telephone numbers or make a note on the phone numbers list that gives the location of the folder. For directions, consider using one of the computer programs and printing the driving directions as well as a map. Also consider having a first aid kit in an easily identifiable place rather than having items in a medicine cabinet.

DOCTOR'S NAME AND TELEPHONE NUMBER

DOCTOR'S OFFICE LOCATION AND DIRECTIONS

MEDICAL INSURANCE NAME AND POLICY NUMBER

DENTIST'S NAME AND TELEPHONE NUMBER

DENTIST'S OFFICE LOCATION AND DIRECTIONS

DENTAL INSURANCE NAME AND POLICY NUMBER

By Child:

_____
NAME

_____
ALLERGIES

_____
ANY PREVIOUS REACTIONS TO MEDICATIONS

_____
REGULAR MEDICATIONS

_____
BLOOD TYPE

_____
ANY OTHER SPECIAL NOTES

_____
DATE OF POWER OF ATTORNEY (IF NEEDED)

THE "GET-AROUND-TO-IT" LIST

Note: Break projects out by those that take a combined effort and those that can be done with minimal supervision. Make a sheet for each project. Children can make their own or you can help. If you are in a family where separation is a routine occurrence, think about creating a "Get-Around-To-It" notebook, and keep it handy.

_____
PROJECT

_____
TOOLS/EQUIPMENT (IF NEEDED)

_____
OTHER SUPPLIES

_____
HOW MANY PEOPLE NEEDED

_____
AGES THAT CAN DO THE PROJECT

_____
HOW MUCH TIME EXPECTED TO TAKE (HOURS OR DAYS)

WHAT DID YOU BRING ME?

Note: This can be a "Get-Around-To-It" project, and each child can create a standing "wish list" that can be updated periodically. For older children and teens, an online effort such as Amazon.com uses might be ideal. Or an adult can fill out the wish list for a younger child.

By Person

_____
NAME

_____
SHIRT/BLOUSE SIZE

_____
DRESS/PANTS SIZE

_____
HAT SIZE

_____
SWEATER SIZE

_____
COLLECTIONS/HOBBIES

_____
ONLINE GIFT REGISTERS (SUCH AS AMAZON.COM)

DESCRIPTION OF AMAZON.COM WISH LIST AND INSTRUCTIONS

[Note: Other online retailers have similar programs. The selection of Amazon.com as a specific example is to provide information; it is not an endorsement.]

From the Amazon.com homepage (www.amazon.com), select the Wish List Tab. You will find a menu that takes you into greater detail. The key areas below are directly from the site:

WISH LISTS:

Wish Lists are a great way for people to let others know the things they would most like to own. They also make it easy to ensure that the gift gets sent to the right place and that the recipient doesn't receive more than he or she wants. Some people create Wish Lists a few months before they are going to have a birthday. Others create them for no particular reason other than the fact that some kind soul might come along and buy something for them. However you use them, as a gift giver or gift recipient, we hope that you find Wish Lists a useful service.

MAKING SURE SOMEONE HASN'T ALREADY BOUGHT AN ITEM:

Gift givers can see which items have already been purchased off someone else's Wish List by looking at the Received column. If the requested number of a particular item have already been purchased, that item will automatically move to the bottom of the list under the heading "The following items have already been purchased."

WHERE PURCHASES ARE SENT:

People who purchase items from a Wish List can opt to send them to whichever address they want, but the default delivery address is the one that the creator of the Wish List provides when the list is created. Gift givers can see only the name, city, and state associated with this address. The street address remains hidden. It's easy to change the address to which purchases from your Wish List are sent.

CREATING A WISH LIST:

It's easy to create a Wish List. Just shop in any area of our store. When you find an item you would like to add to your Wish List, click the "Add to my Wish List" button. You'll find it under the "Add to my Shopping Cart" button on any item's detail page.

Next, click the "Create" button so that you can provide your name and shipping address for any gifts that are ordered for you. (Don't worry—people looking at your Wish List will be able to see only the city and state portion of your address.)

You can also choose to make your list searchable and to add a description of yourself to help out those searching for your Wish List. (Are you the Bill Smith who likes kayaking and science fiction, or the Bill Smith who is a professional bicyclist allergic to carrots?) You can even choose to provide e-mail addresses of friends and family with whom you would like to share your list, so that we can send them a copy.

Should you ever want to change the shipping address or search information associated with your Wish List, simply click the "Wish List" link at the top of almost any page of our store and then click the appropriate "Edit" button. Sign in with your e-mail address and password, make your changes, and click the "Update" button.

MAKING YOUR WISH LIST SEARCHABLE:

When you create your Wish List, you can choose to make it searchable. A searchable Wish List is easier for your friends and family to find. When you make your list searchable, any Amazon.com user can locate your list by searching for your last name or e-mail address. (Your Wish List will not be searchable until the next business day.) If you choose not to make your Wish List searchable, only those people to whom you send notice of your Wish List will be able to access it. When you create your Wish List, you can provide e-mail addresses of persons with whom you would like to share your list, such as friends or family. We will send those people an e-mail message on your behalf containing a link to your list that will allow them to access the list and purchase items for you. We will use the e-mail addresses you provide for this purpose only, and will never disclose or send promotional e-mail to those e-mail addresses.

FLYING A MINOR UNACCOMPANIED

Making the Decision:

Does the child meet the minimum age requirement? Check with the specific airline. (Ages and other criteria are not standard in the industry.)

Is the child familiar with flying and airport procedures? These are things like checking in, waiting, using the bathroom on an airplane, rules for use of electronic and entertainment items.

Does the child want to fly alone?

Are there potential weather impacts? (Flying to winter-storm prone areas in the winter or tornado/severe thunderstorm areas in the summer.)

Are there potential medication impacts? (Timing of any required medications)

After The Decision is Yes:

Do you have the required contact information on both ends? (Check with the specific airline. Criteria are not standard in the industry.)

Can the person on the other end be contacted for the duration of the flight, or flights, in the event of delay?

Is the child old enough to use a telephone calling card, have a cellular telephone or other communication devices like wireless e-mail? If so, practice beforehand. Have you packed easily accessible items for entertainment and food? Practically speaking, this means an under-the-seat bag—not overhead—so the child doesn't have to ask for help in retrieving the bag.

Will the child be carrying extra cash or a credit card? If so, does the child know how to use it responsibly?

SHOULD I TAKE THE FAMILY ALONG?

What will your schedule be?

Will child care be required? If so, who will handle the arrangements?

Is there a back-up if something goes wrong with the primary?

What medical/dental care is available if needed?

Are there organized children/teen programs? If so, are reservations required?

What is the cost and what does it include?

Will transportation be an issue?

If driving, how familiar is your family with the area?

Are there complicating factors such as heavy traffic or poorly signed roads?

If public transportation is to be used, how accessible is it to the lodging?

How familiar is your family with using the transportation?

What activities are available and easily accessible?

Outdoor:

Amusement/Theme parks

Bicycle/Motorbike areas/Paths

Golf, mini-golf

Guided Tours (vehicle or walking?)

Hiking

Horseback riding

Parks

Tennis

Water Sports (beaches, boating, and pool)

Zoos

Indoor:

Amusement Arcades

Aquariums

Bowling

Cable/In-room video entertainment

Cyber Cafes or other computer access

Gyms/Fitness Centers/Swimming

Libraries

Movie Theaters

Museums, galleries, historical buildings

Shopping

WHEN TO LEAVE A TEEN ALONE OVERNIGHT

How much experience does the teen have with being alone or "latch key"?

Does the teen want to stay alone?

Are there trustworthy relatives nearby?

Are you friendly with the neighbors?

Are there local laws that impact?

Has the teen ever been through, or handled, a medical emergency?

Is your Medical Information Checklist up to date?

Are there pets to be cared for?

What will be your connectivity to home?

How easy will it be if you have to return home early?

Can you leave a spare house or car (if applicable) key with a neighbor or nearby relative?

What are the transportation impacts? If your teen is driving, will the rules be different than when you are at home?

Will after-school activities be affected?

What will the food arrangements be?

What will money arrangements be?

Will there be more than one teen at home?

Will there be special restrictions on friends coming over?

THE EMPTY NEST AS A PLACE TO VISIT

The purpose of this checklist is just to give you a quick idea of some of the things to consider to help your child/children make the transition into independence.

Will you become empty-nesters in stages or all at once?

More than one child at home?

Child going to college, or relocating for job, marriage, military service?

Have you thought seriously about what you and your spouse want to do when you become empty-nesters?

Will an empty nest involve physical changes to your current living arrangements?

New or remodeled house?

Moving to a new location?

Does your teenager/young adult have knowledge of, or experience with, household management details such a setting up a budget and the elements of expenses other than rent and utilities?

Has your teenager/ young adult ever worked at a job for a salary?

Does your teenager/young adult (or you on their behalf) have a debt load from schooling, credit cards, etc.?

Will a lump sum outlay of some kind be required for something like a vehicle, apartment or utility deposits or down payments? If so, is it from you or the teenager/young adult?

If post-departure financial support is required by your teenager/young adult, are you and your spouse in agreement over how that will work?

If your teenager/young adult does return to the empty nest, can you all mutually agree on the conditions for another departure?

PART TWO

Sources and Resources

Background Facts and Studies

I know that not everyone is going to read this book cover to cover, and some won't be interested in the *why* as much as the *what.* I've started with the background facts and studies section for those who like the extra detail. The headings of the different sections are clearly marked for those who want to get right to the point. You can jump from topic to topic. The organizations, programs, and sites sections have some repetition because many of the same ideas and principles are handled with slightly different approaches and nuances.

Department of Defense (DOD), the Military Services, and Families

The old military saying "If Uncle Sam wanted you to have a family, he would have issued you one," has been barked out by more than one gruff veteran, yet when the U.S. government transitioned from a draft military in December 1972 into an All-Volunteer (VOLAR) Force, the issues of families began to emerge as important to retention.

For those who experienced military life from the 1940s through the late 1960s, the shift in the sociological and community climate of the military was gradual. There were few noticeable changes until the full impact of the Vietnam conflict resulted in the decision to do away with the draft. Since eligible men knew they were subject to the draft, many young men chose not to marry until after they had served their required two- to three-year term and the low pay for military personnel was not an issue. The "career" military people tended toward families composed of two parents with a wife who did not work outside the home, and everyone had children. The women were additionally expected to cheerfully provide hundreds of hours of volunteer community service and to support each other while the men were deployed for genuine or simulated combat actions. Not surprisingly, the children were expected to behave and if there were boys, at least one of them would follow "in the old man's footsteps." Coping with the stress of separations was simply not considered as something for the organization as an institution to be concerned with.

The military could ignore nationwide social upheaval and the protests about involvement in Vietnam only to a point. In 1970, the Gates Commission Report from Congress laid out a path for transition from a draft military to an All-Volunteer Force. By 1973, the recommendations became a series of phased-in realities, and one of the realities that emerged was the need to address retention factors. Pay raises, revamped educational benefits, and advertising campaigns shifted the demographics of service personnel within less than a decade. The number of women in the military grew from barely 2 percent to 12 percent by the 1990s; younger soldiers with families entered the force, and military wives began to reflect the national trend, as more took jobs outside the home.[1] The wives who chose the "traditional role" also began to articulate their concerns with what became collectively known as "quality of life issues" (QOL).

Serious studies with analytical data started to replace anecdotal input, and thousands of women who had been expected to "Keep the home fires burning" began to vocalize that a new, more participatory social order was on the way, whether the Department of Defense was ready for it or not. Consequently, initiatives have grown since the 1970s that are designed specifically to help families adjust to aspects of military life such as frequent or prolonged separations. Each service—the Army, Air Force, Navy, Marine Corps, Coast Guard, and the Reserve Component/National Guard of the services—has its own programs, and the Department of Defense has additional, overarching programs available.

The studies I have highlighted were located and obtained primarily though the Military Family Resource Center, an organization that I will discuss in the section on Programs, Support Organizations and Helpful Sites.

VOICES THAT SPOKE AND WERE HEARD

A handful of articles were circulated in the mid-1940s that centered on the topics of military personnel and the impact of their absences on the families who waited for their return. It can be easily understood, however, that these early observations were not given a high priority, considering the tumultuous events surrounding War World II and the subsequent shift into a Cold War nuclear arms race. Medical personnel, psychologists, family counselors, and some clergy were the predominant individuals who began documenting concerns during the late 1960s. There was an exponential leap in this area of research that began in 1973 and continues on a regular basis.

The relationship of the family to the well-being of the military member could no longer be ignored, and in 1977, the American Psychological Association conducted the first symposium devoted exclusively to the military family. Several studies grouped into the package, *Changing Families in a Changing Military System*, edited by Edna J. Hunter of the Naval Health Research Center in San Diego, California, was the focal point of the symposium. The studies dealt with multiple topics, although the impact of separation was obviously high on the list. The following is an extract from the introduction:

> Military personnel have always felt the impact of numerous transitions— from civilian to military status, from peace to combat to peace, from one assignment to another, from one geographic area to another, and from active military status to retirement. The military family, too, has experienced the effects of war, mobility, separations and loss. Only recently, however, has the military system begun to feel the impact of the military family. Whenever sudden dramatic changes or transitions occur, crises may result either for the individual or the institution. At the present time both the military system and the military family are in a period of rapid transition. Perhaps one of the most important changes that has occurred

within the military since World War II has been the change from a "single-man's" Army to a married-man's Army, Navy or Air Force.

A more recent change is the growing acceptance of women service personnel as an integral part of the military structure. With the increasing numbers of women affiliated with the military—wives of servicemen and husbands of servicewomen included—their importance to the military and their impact upon the military organization increases proportionately—perhaps even more than proportionately, when the ingredient of the changing role of women in society in general is added to the equation for change.

. . . The mere fact that this symposium—the first symposium at the American Psychological Association meetings devoted exclusively to the military family—was even scheduled is evidence of the growing recognition of the importance of the military family within an all-volunteer force and its importance in relation to recruitment, job performance, job satisfaction, and retention in the service.[2]

Anyone who is familiar with government bureaucracy will also be aware that despite some of the phrases above, there was no sudden implementation of what later became a series of independent, and sometimes connected, family support programs. There are always reasons for delays: funding is critical, trying to determine the best approach; trying to determine how to staff such programs, etc.

More articles appeared and studies increased during the 1980s, including articles such as *Paternal Separation and the Military Dependent Child* by Lieutenant Colonel Gentry W. Yeatman, of the Medical Corps:

Paternal separation due to the non-accompanied tour presents significant problems for the military family. It is not unusual for the medical pediatrician to see children with various somatic complaints or disciplinary problems which start abruptly with the departure of the father. The mother and child may be under significant emotional stress.

While extreme hardship cases are most easily remembered, it is obvious that the majority of separated tours do not require medical intervention. Furthermore, it is impossible to provide concurrent travel to all duty stations. In order to help determine the prevalence and severity of behavioral and somatic problems exhibited by the children of the separated serviceman, a retrospective questionnaire was developed.[3]

Lt. Col. Yeatman described the methodology of the study, and after they sorted through the respondents, only one hundred fit the criteria of the serviceman who were, or had been assigned to, a lengthy, yet noncombat-related separation and had children. While the sample was small, the results were added to the growing amount of analytical data that indicated the military as an institution needed to step forward.

Separation problems occurred at any age over 12 months without a clear sex preference. While the majority of problems surrounding a separation of the father were not severe and were transient in nature, several families had significant problems requiring professional help. Readjustment after return of the father, though usually mild, was on several occasions marked by fear and resentment of several months duration. The child less than two years old was at greatest risk.

. . . As might be expected, the Serviceman was less likely to be aware of problems at home during separation, less likely to admit them, or more prone to forget them. While two-thirds of wives felt that problems existed, only one-third of Servicemen were aware of problems.

. . . Of 100 families who had experienced an unaccompanied tour, 66 reported a problem with at least one child. Of 152 children from those families 51 (34 percent) had disciplinary problems, 28 (19 per cent) experienced phobias, and 17 (11 percent) had a fall in school grades. Multiple somatic complaints, poor self-image and a feeling of punishment were not uncommon. There was no clustering of symptoms at a given age or sex.

. . . The non-accompanied tour is related to problems of a significant nature in many children and a serious nature in a few. Although many other factors are involved, the separation itself clearly correlates well (at least temporarily) with significant aberrant social behavior. Although most children seem to recover from the effects of sudden paternal separation, some children seem to be at risk for severe permanent behavioral disorders.[4]

A 1992 article by Wayne Blount, Amos Curry, and Gerald I. Lubin echoed the need for institutional level involvement as was stated in these key points:

Family separations are an intrinsic part of military life. The temporary loss of a family member through deployment brings unique stresses to a family in three different stages; predeployment, survival and reunion. Most families adapt to these stresses well; however, families who do not have adequate coping skills can experience problems as a result of these stresses. Health care providers must be aware of these stresses, the factors placing families at risk, the clinical manifestations of these stresses and the techniques for preventing and treating them. The clinical presentations of stress-related medical problems most often involves depressive symptoms in both adults and children. Families at the most risk for manifesting family separation stresses are those with a history of poor adapting skills, poor predeployment attitudes, family conflicts, dysfunctional family relationships, and poor communication. In addition, young spouses, lower pay grade personnel and foreign spouses are at an increased risk for separation problems. Prevention is best sought through family support groups.[5]

As of March 2002, there were almost 150 reports and studies in the databank maintained by the Military Family Resource Center (MRFC) that address factors of family separation. Military members, family members, various professional experts, military leaders at all levels, and members of Congress were speaking out and looking for ways to positively affect a concern that was no longer to be brushed aside.

The tone of Lt. Col. Yeatman's article is heavier than most of what I am discussing throughout the book, but the U.S. military leadership does have a tendency to be what is politely termed "mission-focused," and it took nearly a decade for the concept of the family as a component of readiness to take hold. Once the idea was articulated in those terms, fledgling programs and structured support offices found a foothold in the military jargon. The mobilization of more than 316,000 Reserve Component personnel during Operations Desert Shield and Desert Storm genuinely gave rise to the need for better cooperation between the services and the families. Approximately 541,000 total U.S. military personnel were deployed to the Gulf Region from the August 1990 invasion to the victory parades in the summer of 1991.

The wives, husbands, and other relatives who "kept the home fires burning" this time turned to the leadership both during and after the Gulf War and provided input as to the good, not-so-good, and downright inefficient aspects of some of the ideas.

TECHNOLOGY AND
RAISING EXPECTATIONS

As far as the military was concerned, mobile telephone and sophisticated satellite communications were for battlefield enhancements
with far less frequent use aimed at service member morale. But once
the technology genie is out of the proverbial bottle (and okay, combined with the entrepreneurial spirit and capitalism), multiple applications inevitably follow.

Dr. Morton G. Ender, a noted scholar of military sociology, has
authored numerous papers, and in 1997, he released *E-mail to
Somalia: New Communication Media Between Home and War-Fronts.* One
chapter of this lengthy work details the 1993 official e-mail program
established to connect the deployed U.S. military personnel with
their families. From the initial deployment to Somalia, East Africa, in
December 1992 to the spring of 1994, Operation Restore Hope
involved 25,000 U.S. service personnel (10,000 Army, 10,000
Marines, 4,000 Navy, and 1,000 Air Force) as well as 13,000 other
service members from twenty different countries.[6]

The pilot program lasted for thirteen months and was governed
by several rules and restrictions in typical military fashion: a required
form for messages to be typed on, a word limit, etc., and the message
was retyped for transmission. Despite the restrictions, a total of 9,435
messages were processed with 5,760 sent from family and 3,675 sent
by service members. The bottom line was that the majority of partic-
ipants viewed the program to be successful, albeit in need of
improvement. Dr. Ender's research revealed the emergent themes of
speed, privacy, decentralization, and personal communication. The
following segments from different parts of Dr. Ender's work synthe-
size two major points:

Speed:

Throughout the history of military operations, soldiers and family
members have consistently sought communication media to help overcome isolation and separation. An attribute of communication technology across this history has been a process of time and space reduction. For
example, the amount of time required for a letter to travel across the
United States continent via pony express could take one month.

Mechanized power reduced that time in half. Airpower reduced it even more. Electronics and digitalization obliterate time.

. . . Personal Communication Media:

The personal ownership of communication media is important to American soldiers and their families. Almost all of the family members and soldiers in the present study used an array of both old and new media. Fifty percent of the soldiers and the family members in this study own computers and modems. . . . Likewise, the purchase of communications in the civilian society continues unabated into the latter part of this century. Almost all military post exchanges around the world provide electronic communication devices commercially, and at some reduced price, for soldiers and their families. This trend toward owning and using of personal communication media is expected to continue into the 21st century.

Another issue is indirect access to personal communication media. . . . Even the soldiers and their families not owning personal high tech media have been touched by it in the workplace. A likely future scenario in a military community could involve using communication media at work or a community computer and modem shared among neighbors in a military housing area.[7]

GETTING THE WORD OUT

Dr. Ender's work and that of many more have indeed helped shape the kinds of programs that Department of Defense and the individual services have adopted. There are two important notes, though, before I get into describing some of the support available to military members and families.

The first point is that while accessibility to communications technology has dramatically increased, personal ownership is often still limited due to either geographical location or lower pay among junior members of the services. This is why locations have been established in a significant number of military communities to provide at least periodic, if not day-to-day, access.

The second point is that information about the programs continues to lag behind the availability of programs. A 1999 Navy Leadership Survey indicated that senior leaders were more familiar with family support programs than were junior leaders and that the lack of program awareness is the top reason for nonuse.[8]

As a long-time user of military programs, I fully acknowledge that there is almost always room for improvement, and the best of intentions can get bogged down in frustrating bureaucratic nonsense. Notwithstanding those opinions, the military has made great strides, and I hope that this book will in some measure help familiarize people with the expansion of services and support.

PROGRAMS, SUPPORT ORGANIZATIONS, AND HELPFUL SITES

With that said, let's take a look at a multitude of organizations where parents or children can locate useful information or interact with others who also deal with the issues surrounding balancing family and work-related travel. Information-packed websites pop up (and disappear) on a regular basis; the ones listed in these sections are some that I either have personal knowledge of or that have been established for several years.

And no, I haven't forgotten my promise—the corporate world is also represented for anyone who might want to slide past the military part. The primary difference in the corporate world is that there is no nationwide "leadership" entity, and that has good points as well as drawbacks. While there may not be a large body to "focus and centralize efforts," that also means corporations and individual companies can be more flexible in their design and approach, and individuals can often negotiate business-related travel or something like telecommuting options. The corporate world is often decidedly more reasonable about travel arrangements in areas such as allowing larger expense accounts so parents can choose lodging accommodations that cater to the traveling parent.

There are thousands of stories of businesses that refuse to acknowledge the impact of work-related travel on families, but there are those that are listening and trying to work within profit-making requirements, while still allowing their employees latitude in how they operate. The profusion of electronic-based communication gadgetry has certainly helped, and the routine use of computer and

Internet access has opened the door even further for sites such as Bluesuitmom.com. Bluesuitmom is discussed later in this section.

If you view the military side first, you might get some extra ideas or you can skim through that and pinpoint the area that interests you the most.

OFFICIAL MILITARY PROGRAMS AND WEBSITES

The Department of Defense homepage, http://www.defenselink.mil, is open to anyone. There is a list of links for each of the military services, or you can click on the Family link that then provides access to all the sites discussed in the official section. Additionally, there is a section, DeploymentLink, that contains a special Kids Information on Deployment Stuff (K.I.D.S) section among other items. It is divided into Grades K–4, 5–8 and 9–12 and covers subjects such as geography, culture, etc., about the regions where U.S. military personnel are deployed.

The official programs, however, are not exclusively web-based since that would defeat the purpose of trying to reach the greatest number of eligible personnel. Mailing addresses and telephone numbers are provided for individuals who do not have easy access to a military installation.

THE MILITARY FAMILY RESOURCE (MFRC)

This is the only organization/site that I have included that is not advice-based. It is, instead, a central repository for people who are charged with developing and managing family programs or conducting research. The following is from the About Us page that can be accessed at http://mfrc.calib.com:

> The Military Family Resource Center (MFRC) is a tool for enhancing the effectiveness of military family policy and programs. MFRC's mission is to act as a catalyst of information between the Department of Defense Military Community and Family Policy (MCFP) office and military policy makers and program staff and to deliver timely, efficient, and effective information services through cutting-edge technology.

HOW . . . through our E-mail alerts, we advise you of new publications and events. Review the Policy and Special Issues selections of the MFRC Website to learn of new policies and to obtain tools that will enhance your programs. Review our Research and Model Programs section for the latest on military family issues. Search our Online Databases to find documents related to military quality of life issues. Download publications, information and resources on our Publications page.

MRFC also incorporates the National Clearinghouse for the Military Child Development Program. The Clearinghouse was created by the Department of Defense in response to the President's urging that the lessons learned from the Military Child Development Program be widely shared with the rest of the nation to improve the quality of child care in the United States. While this remains the central issue, the focus of the Clearinghouse has been expanded to include information on military youth programs.

Military Family Resource Center
CS4, Suite 302, Room 309
1745 Jefferson Davis Hwy.
Arlington, VA 22202-3424
Phone: (703) 602-4964
DSN: 332-4964
E-mail:mfrcrequest@calib.com

MILITARY TEENS ON THE MOVE (MTOM)

MTOM is a part of the Military Assistance Program, although it is only a website. It is designed to address issues and concerns primarily for ages ten and older. There is a brief survey to fill out prior to entering the site, but, once inside, there are chat rooms and easy-to-use icons that link into areas of special interest to older children and teens, with a dedicated icon for dealing with deployment. Enter through http://www.defenselink.mil and click on Family for MTOM.

AIR FORCE SPECIFIC—CROSSROADS

This is the section of the Air Force website that is focused on family and community issues and is subdivided into different categories that range from parenting to eldercare. Log onto www.af.mil and click on Crossroads. The following is the introduction paragraph:

> Welcome to the Air Force Crossroads section on Family Separation and Readiness! This section is dedicated to those members and their families and friends who are separated due to deployments, remote assignments, extended TDYs [temporary duty], natural disasters, and professional military education requirements. While separation can be a difficult experience for members and their families and friends, the Air Force is dedicated to providing our people quality service to make it as painless as possible. The information and resources provided here can make the experience a positive one for you and your family.

Three specific sections are the Spouse Network, the Communications Center, and Family Separation:

> Welcome to the Air Force Crossroads' Spouse Network! The Air Force recognizes the importance of the military spouse and the unique challenges specific to that role. This section of the site is designed specifically for you. It provides a means of communication and access to resources and information Air Force-wide on a variety of topics affecting spouses and their families. Today's global Air Force often calls upon the military member to perform his or her duties away from home, leaving the spouse alone to maintain the family unit. It is the intent of the Spouse Network to assist spouses with the daily routine as well as those extraordinary circumstances that inevitably seem to occur when the sponsor is away and the spouse is responsible for total management of home and family. Spouses are invited to become a member of the Spouse Network and to learn from each other, sharing experiences, information and resources from both home and abroad.

> Welcome to the Communications Center section of Air Force Crossroads! The Air Force knows how important it is to stay in touch. Because of our mobile life styles, we want to provide you every opportunity to get the information you need, stay in touch with friends and loved ones and communicate across the miles.

> This Communication Center contains a variety of forums/conference boards available for communication between Air Force spouses, teens and other selected groups. We are also in the process of developing an

online video teleconferencing capability that will allow you to have video contact with family members across the country and around the globe.

The Family Separation section contains a lengthy and useful *Predeployment Guide: A Tool For Coping.* The following is an extract from Section I: Predeployment/ General:

> Too often, family members deny the possibility of duty separation, and pretend it is not going to happen. This denial can be emotionally harmful. Once separation occurs, they are likely to find themselves unprepared. It is much healthier for families to face issues directly and become better prepared to positively address the life style changes brought about by separation. Adequate preparation for all family members is the key to minimizing the problems which will inevitably arise during a duty separation. Sometimes families avoid talking about things which bother or worry them. They are afraid that talking about things will make matters worse. In reality, open discussion provides family members the opportunity to clarify potential misunderstandings, get a better idea of what is expected, work out solutions to identified problems, and to better prepare themselves for the coming separation.
>
> . . . There is a difference between being ready 'to go,' and ready 'to part.' Being ready 'to go' means having your duffel bag packed, all shots up to date, and other duty essential preparations completed. Being ready 'to part' from your spouse and other family members means being aware of the personal and family issues related to separation, and being prepared to deal as constructively as possible with those issues.

Section II, Children Issues, covers many of the areas already discussed, but there are a couple of extra thoughts and good ideas. The below passages are only part of Section II:

> VISIT YOUR CHILD'S TEACHER. Frequently children react to the assignment or deployment by misbehaving in class or performing poorly in their studies. A teacher who is aware of the situation is in a better position to be sensitive and encouraging.
>
> HELP CHILDREN TO PLAN FOR THE DEPARTURE. While the spouse is packing their bags, allow your children to assist you in some way. Suggest a "swap" of some token, something of your child's that can be packed in a duffel bag in return for something that belongs to the departing spouse.

Discuss the household chores and let your children choose (as much as possible) the ones they would rather do. Mother and Father need to agree with each other that division of household chores is reasonable. The role of disciplinarian needs to be supported by the departing member.

BEING A LONG DISTANCE PARENT. Parenting while away from home is not easy. Some separated parents find it so emotionally difficult they withdraw and become significantly less involved in the lives of their children while they are apart. This, of course, is not good either for the parent or the children, not to mention the difficulty it causes the parent/caregiver who is at home alone. The most important aspect of parenting from a distance is making those small efforts to stay in touch. Doing something to say the parent is thinking about and missing the child is what is most important.

ARMY SPECIFIC— THE U.S. ARMY FAMILY LIAISON (FLO)

The Army Family Liaison Office (AFLO) was established to act as the honest broker for the Army family. The staff is dedicated to fostering well-being for Army families, serves as the Ombudsman, and communicates with the greater Army on the subject of family issues. They provide information about all aspects of military life, and their site contains numerous links to the other services as well as listings to many unofficial organizations. The site has expanded considerably during the past few years and is continuously adding new listings in response to feedback. The Smart Book section of the website is especially useful, although it is still growing. FLO also produces a hard copy monthly newsletter. For more information check their site at www.hqda.army.mil/acsim/family (or go through www.defenselink.mil), call Toll Free at 1-800-833-6622, or write to:

The Army Family Liaison Office
Office, ACSIM
600 Army Pentagon
Washington, D.C. 20310-0600

FAMILY READINESS GROUPS (FRG)

One of the initiatives that resulted from the Army's closer look at family issues is establishment of Family Readiness Groups at installations around the globe. It is a support system for soldiers, family members, and units, often most active during periods of separation, field exercises, annual training, deployment, and all levels of mobilization. The two primary goals of FRGs are to open channels of communication to pass correct information between the military chain of command, the families, service organizations like the Red Cross, Army Community Service, etc., and to reduce social isolation by making contact with all families of soldiers and attempt to draw them in and make them feel a part of the Army family.

ARMY FAMILY TEAM BUILDING (AFTB)

Additionally, the Army Family Team Building program, a sequential training program for soldiers, civilians, and their family members, has been designed to provide skills and knowledge for living successfully within the unique framework of Army life. The intent of the training is to improve personal and family preparedness, which in turn enhances overall Army readiness. AFTB is taught to active duty and reserve component soldiers, and certain Department of the Army civilians. Classes for family members are not mandatory, but all family members will gain insights into the Army way of life, experience personal growth and may earn college credit through attendance. AFTB does not replace existing programs, but, rather, is an additional resource to organizations such as the Army Community Service, Family Advocacy Programs, Family Readiness Groups, Family Life Programs, and mayoral programs. These are part of the support structure that has been developed to assist soldiers and their families, much like the programs found in many hometowns.

The Family Readiness Groups and the Army Family Team Building Program do not have specific addresses since they are in place at most Army installations. They can be found in the list of the Services and Support and/or Family Organization section of installation information. Families who are new to the Army, whether active duty or in a reserve status, are especially encouraged to attend the classes or respond to at least initial invitations to the Family Readiness Groups.

THE U.S. NAVY AND
THE U.S. MARINE CORPS

Sea duty for Navy personnel and the Expeditionary Forces mission training for the Marine Corps ensures routine, months-long deployments even during times of peace. The Navy Lifelinks segment can be reached through either defenselink.mil or at http://www. lifelines2000.org. The menu contains several sections to include one on Family Life and a separate one for Deployment Readiness. The following is from the introduction to Deployment Readiness:

> The Deployment Readiness section can help you and your family prepare for and cope with the stresses associated with tours of duty.
>
> The Navy and Marine Corps understand the questions and worries that arise as you prepare for a deployment—often to remote parts of the globe. With the help of deployment and family services experts, we have developed some helpful resources to provide answers to your questions, and to lessen the strain on you and your family.

The section is then subdivided into Pre-Deployment, Mid-Deployment, Post Deployment, Overseas Deployment, and Reserve Recalls/Mobilizations segments that focus on the specific actions needed for each part of the Deployment phases. There are articles about a wide variety of topics such as "The 7 Emotional Cycles of Deployments" or "Homecoming Celebrations: A Fun Tradition!" The articles are changed regularly and, of course, families can pose specific questions and find additional sources if they cannot find the information they are seeking on the site.

THE RESERVE COMPONENTS—
RESERVE AND NATIONAL GUARD

Each of the military services has corresponding Reserve Components that are made up of men and women who spend a portion of each year training in their designated fields as individuals and units to perform duties when called up by the proper authorities. These valuable units are a part of the Total Force along with the active duty personnel and Department of Defense civilians. The following is from the 27 March 2002 Department of Defense News Release:

> At any given time, Services may mobilize some units and individuals while demobilizing others, making it possible for these figures to either increase or decrease. Total number currently on active duty in support of the partial mobilization for the Army National Guard and Army Reserve is 28,389; Naval Reserve, 10,597; Air National Guard and Air Force Reserve, 35,981; Marine Corps Reserve, 4,396; and the Coast Guard Reserve 1,830. This brings the total Reserve and National Guard on active duty to 81,193 from 50 states, the District of Columbia, Puerto Rico and individual augmentees.[9]

While each of the military services includes Reserve Component tabs on their sites, there is also a separate site that can be accessed either through defenselink.mil or by logging onto http://www.defenselink.mil/ra/.

As mentioned previously, hundreds of thousands of Reserve Component personnel were mobilized during the Gulf War, and the unique needs of their families have recently been recognized at the highest echelons of leadership. The following three sections from the site contain comments that speak to this commitment:

The DOD Family Readiness Challenge:

The Guard and Reserve are essential to our Nation's daily worldwide defense operations. Their contributions are no longer limited to times of national mobilization, but are instead critical to our very ability to project power. The Total Force integration policy has created a seamless force with the mobility and flexibility we need to meet the challenges of a still-dangerous world. Guard and Reserve contributions have not been without cost. In the past three years, Reservists have contributed an annual average of nearly 13 million duty days to Total Force Mission.

Family readiness and mission readiness are inextricably linked. Families play a vital role in the reenlistment decision. Families that are unprepared to withstand the stress of deployment or active duty for training will ultimately impact on unit morale and retention.

The challenge for commanders and senior leaders is to build a partnership among service members, unit leaders, families and the community. That partnership must prepare and sustain families before, during and after periods of active duty.

The DOD Family Readiness Response: Initiatives:

The *National Guard & Reserve Family Readiness Strategic Plan 2000–2005* published in January 2000 calls for a strong, proactive approach to preparing family members of Guard & Reserve personnel for those periods of time when their service members will be separated from them due to military service. A *Guide to Reserve Family Member Benefits* was published in 1999. Both of these documents clearly demonstrate the commitment of the Department of Defense to Guard and Reserve family readiness.

As the next step, a new joint Guard & Reserve Family Readiness Toolkit has been developed as a guide for commanders, service members, family members and family readiness group leaders and volunteers to enhance family readiness. Mission readiness and family readiness are inextricably intertwined and the Readiness Toolkit capitalizes on a joint standardized approach to readiness. This toolkit will fill a void for the 1.2 million Guard and Reserve men and women who represent one-half of the Total Force. They are critical contributors to every mission and essential to our national security.

Readiness Toolkit: Your Mobility Resource:

The newly published *Guard & Reserve Family Readiness Toolkit* highlights the best practices and models from all seven Guard and Reserve components refined into a joint standardized format. Specifically the toolkit includes:

Standardized pre-deployment and mobilization checklists

Sample Command and Family Readiness Group Newsletters

Standard Forms (Record of Personal Affairs, Family Information . . .)

Publicity Protocols

Family Readiness Group Guides, Training Materials, and Volunteer Management

Healthcare Information (TRICARE)

Employer Support Information

Personal Financial Management

Legal Affairs

Special Interest Topics (Parent Education Information, Separations, Reunions, Elder Care)

Resources and Useful Websites

Outcome Measures and Survey Instruments

While the above programs and sites fall under the official umbrella of the services, there are other sites/organizations that are unofficial but great resources, described below.

Unofficial, but Service-Related— Plenty to Share

THE MILITARY BRAT NETWORK

The Military Brat Network was designed by a former Military Brat who wanted to reach out to those who sometimes feel they don't really have a voice (or an ear for that matter). The network hosts *On the Move*, a newsletter packed with brat news, stories, articles, and photographs, announcements, and classifieds. *On The Move* is the only publication devoted entirely to all Military Brats, stateside and overseas. It provides information and a forum for articles written by older children and teens, as well as adults. The site also welcomes former military brats who may no longer be affiliated with the military, but who do want to pass along advice or just reminiscences. For more information check their site www.militarybrats.com or write to:

Military Brat Network
PO Box 956541
Duluth, GA 30095-6541

SERGEANT MOMS

This is an Internet-only site, but it is jammed with useful information and links. I've been corresponding with the current "SGTMOM" for the past couple of years. Carrie Gissiner, who deserves more recognition than I can give for what she's done in a nonpaying capacity, is an ordinary person in the sense that she entered into an endeavor in a strictly grassroots way. I've included a section about the site here, and if you read Chapter Ten, Stories From Around, you may have seen Carrie's input about life as a Navy family. This is an especially useful site for someone who is new to the military. Here's Carrie's description of her site and the history behind it:

> Welcome to Sgtmoms! I've been a Navy wife for almost 19 years now—officially 19 on Aug 13th! We have a 16-year-old son and a 13-year-old daughter. (Yes, we've hit the really fun stage!)
>
> Sgt. Mom's Place was begun in late 1995 by an Army wife. In early 1996 I came across the site and became friends with the owner. I began to help answer e-mails and questions for her shortly after that. By 1997 the original Sgt. Mom decided to homeschool her kids. Originally she was going to just let the site die a slow death and drop off the web once her domain registration was up.
>
> My husband and I agreed this site was too much of a positive thing for military families for it to disappear; it was and is such a wonderful resource, we didn't want to see it end. I talked with my husband in detail about taking over the site because I knew it would be a major "time sucker." It's nothing for me to spend 40 hours a week on the site and e-mails. Some weeks are much better and it's only about 15–20 hours. And this is all out of pocket. So then I broached the idea with the original Sgt. Mom, she mulled it over and asked if I wanted to buy the domain. I did, and I guess you could say the rest is history. I have had it since and at times it's been a wild ride. I'm currently working on a new format for the site and hope to have it up and running soon.
>
> It has grown so much in the time I've had it. I've seen my audience change gradually over time: I seem to have many more parents visiting now, as well as spouses. These parents have their son or daughter go off to basic and have no idea what their child is doing or what they have ahead of them, and the parents want to know what to expect. The events of September 11, 2001, forced a drastic rise in hits to the site as well as e-mails with questions and people wanting some sort of reassurance. I am also seeing many more visits from spouses of Reserve soldiers. So many Reservists are being activated for homeland security and many of their spouses have not really had to deal with the military. Many of them are used to one weekend a month and two weeks a year, and that is the extent of their contact with the military. Now they are trying to learn to

cope and deal with the separation regular military spouses deal with on a day-to-day basis.

In 2000 I got some official recognition for my site when the DOD [Department of Defense] invited me to speak at the DOD QOL [Quality of Life] Symposium in Seattle, Washington. It was an interesting trip, and I had a great time meeting some of the people I have had e-mail contact with over the years. I spoke at several "break out" sessions and was recognized by the keynote speaker during the opening forum. (It was a bit overwhelming to have a lieutenant general talk about me and have me stand to be recognized by a crowd of more than 700.)

I guess you could say I'm the "Dear Abby" of the military. I'm willing to answer any questions that come my way, if I am able. I've dealt with very serious issues such as suicidal spouses. I've dealt with questions about helping kids cope, trying to make parents understand that their son cannot come home for his sister's wedding because his unit is in the middle of a war zone, and helping teachers with classes wanting to send letters to our service members.

I actually ran across *sgtmoms* when I was the editor for a community newsletter, and I was surprised at the sheer volume of information and the informal way in which it was presented. The strength of this site is that, while there is an undeniable service-orientation, it is definitely not a "speak-the-party-line" site. Log onto www.sgtmoms.com and take a tour for yourself.

THE BUSINESS AND CORPORATE WORLD— ROAD WARRIORS AND OTHER TRAVELERS

I was delighted to have received at least some input from the male perspective about traveling and family issues. Double standards exist in many areas of our culture, and men who want to take a more active role in parenting often find that they are not immune to hard choices when it comes to careers and family obligations. Susanne Braun Levine wrote about this reality in her April 2000 article, *The Good Daddy.* She chronicles several men who are trying to help reverse the perception of the father who wants to make changes.

Today's employers call themselves family-friendly, and for women, that's increasingly true. But men are still expected to make work their top priority.

According to a recent report by the Families and Work Institute, a New York City-based organization that studies workplace issues, some 56 percent of 1,057 companies say that they offer 'employee assistance programs to help workers deal with problems that may affect their personal lives.' But men are less likely than women to avail themselves of these opportunities. Those in the know pass the word that it's better to call in sick than to take a 'family day.' Or, when a child is born, it's smarter to take vacation days than paternity leave.

Surely employed fathers are entitled to the same options as working mothers. The few men and countless women who take advantage of flextime, job sharing and other benefits know that their decision may slow their careers. But women can count on respect, if not support for their choices; men cannot.

For a man, it's still professionally risky to behave in any way that suggests that work is not a top priority. This puts the working father in a dark and lonely place that's difficult to escape from because it's solitary confinement. There aren't many accounts of life behind the wall of silence, where men keep their real priorities, because anyone who wants to be a father 'on company time' quickly learns that he can do so only by flying below the radar. The good news is that there are more and more dedicated dads working and living in a wide range of circumstances.[10]

With this acknowledgement in mind, I'll begin with the organization I found through Dads At A Distance.

The National Long Distance Relationship Building Institute

All right, I have to admit that I found out about this series of sites through the Navy site, but as soon as I logged onto daads.com, I felt as though I had hit the proverbial gold mine. I was concerned that I was tipped too heavily toward the military, and I was fascinated by the idea of an organization devoted to the issue of long distance relationships. One of the founders, Aaron Larson, gave me some of the background:

He and eight other colleagues established the Institute in 1998.

Their formal educational background is in child and family studies and they actually developed the resources when they were working with personnel who were incarcerated. The overwhelming responses to the first sites emphasized the desire of many people for support and information about how to cope with long distance relationships. Additional sites have been added as time permitted. The Institute is currently only Internet-based, although they hope someday to be able to develop a curriculum that can be used for workshops.

The series of sites are: Dads at a Distance, Moms Over Miles, Long Distance Couples, and Grandparenting from a Distance. Each site is linked, so you can access any of them and easily click over to the next one or other recommended sites. I've taken the introduction from the Dads at a Distance homepage, although each site is set up in a similar way. (I've reformatted the sections into straight text without the graphics.)

The Dads at a Distance website has been designed to help fathers who are business travelers, military men, noncustodial fathers, airline pilots, travel guides, traveling salesmen, railroad workers, truckers, professional athletes, musicians/entertainers, actors, corporate executives and any other fathers who have to be away from their children.

Relationships with children are much like plants, they need constant nourishing. At home, this type of nourishment comes easily through the activities and time spent with your children. However, when you are away, this becomes more difficult to accomplish.

This is why we have built this website for long distance dads. It takes a lot of time and effort to think of fun and creative activities that you can do at a distance with your kids. And extra time isn't something that a lot of us have. We hope you will use these activities and share additional activities that you do with your kids. We can post the activities on our site for the benefit of other long distance dads.

We know how hectic life can be in the middle of the week. Sometimes the last thing on your mind is nurturing the relationships with your children who are at a distance. This is why we are offering a free e-mail reminding service. Each Wednesday we will send you a quick reminder to do one of the long distance activities that day with your child. In addition, we will send a suggestion or two that usually takes 5 minutes or less to complete. If you are interested please sign up.

Site addresses are:

www.daads.com
www.momsovermiles.com
www.longdistancegrandparenting.com

Parents Without Partners

I haven't spent a great deal of time talking about the needs of the single parent, but I will always have a special feeling for the additional tasks that face this part of parenting. There are conscious decisions and unavoidable situations that result in single-parent households, and statistics from the U.S. Census Bureau show a decline of two-parent homes since 1980, although the figures have been relatively stable since 1996. Seventy-seven percent of American children lived with two parents in 1980; that dropped to 69 percent by the year 2000. There is a mix of parenting arrangements to include predominantly joint-custody parenting. Twenty-two percent of the children live only with their mothers, 4 percent live only with their fathers and 4 percent live with neither parent.[11]

Parents Without Partners (PWP) understands the unique challenges that can sometimes seem overwhelming to a single parent. I can comfortably suggest that any single parent who is seeking, or even thinking about, a support organization should look into Parents Without Partners. I corresponded briefly with Barbara Spade, the international vice president of community relations. She, like others within the organization, continues to try and let single parents everywhere know that PWP has a wide variety of services to offer. The following is an extract from their site. I've reformatted the text from the mission statement and the history of the organization:

> Parents Without Partners provides single parents and their children with an opportunity for enhancing personal growth, self-confidence and sensitivity towards others by offering an environment for support, friendship and the exchange of parenting techniques.
>
> Parents Without Partners was founded in 1957 in New York City by two single parents: Jim Egleson, a noncustodial parent, and Jacqueline

Bernard, a custodial parent. As concerned parents, they felt isolated from society because of their marital status, and decided to form a mutual support organization. Following their first newspaper advertisements directed to "Parents Without Partners," 25 single parents attended the first meeting in a Greenwich Village church basement. Later, media attention brought inquiries from all over the country.

Parents Without Partners, Inc. is now the largest international, non-profit membership organization devoted to the welfare and interests of single parents and their children. Single parents may join one of approximately 400 chapters; they may be male or female, custodial or noncustodial, separated, divorced, widowed or never-married. Distinct from chapter membership, the affiliate membership is offered to any interested person or business, and the member-at-large membership is offered to any qualified individual. See our 'How to Join Page' for more information on types of membership.

Brief Facts About Parents Without Partners, Inc.

50,000+ members in the United States and Canada.

55% female, 45% male.

Ages range from 18 to 80; most have teenage children.

Average length of membership is four years. Approximately 85% of the membership is separated or divorced.

Never-married members are under-represented in PWP compared to national statistics.

Widowed parent membership is comparable to national statistics.

PWP members are typical middle-class North Americans. They come from all walks of life, representing a kaleidoscope of occupations, interests, and educational attainment.

Some PWP members have only recently become single parents, while others have been single for some time. Some have young children, others have grown children. Some are sophisticated, some have led sheltered lives. All are in a process of transition and change and seek help from PWP.

PWP members are of all faith and political beliefs.

All chapter members are verified as being single parents by members or professionals in the community.

The chapter sizes range from 25 to 1,500 members and all chapters run programs balanced among three areas: Educational activities, Family activities and Adult Social/Recreational activities.

Educational Activities may be group discussions, lectures by psychologists, lawyers and other professionals, study groups, training seminars, leadership and personal growth opportunities.

Family Activities may include holiday activities, potluck suppers, fun and educational outings, picnics, hikes, camping, bowling, etc., for children and their parents. These activities may be unique in that they are the one place where children can be alone with other single parent children.

Adult Social/Recreational Activities help single parents learn to relate again with other adults as single persons.

For more information, check their website at http://www.parentswithoutpartners.org or write to:

Parents Without Partners, Inc
1650 S. Dixie Hwy, Suite 510
Boca Raton, FL 33432

A Woman's Focus

BLUESUITMOM

When I found this robust website, I engaged in e-mail dialog with Rachael Bender and Maria Bailey, its co-founders. It is designed for the working mother, and the strong team has diverse experience with the challenges of work-related separation. Among other areas, there is a newsletter, an ask-an-expert section, and a Daily Stops list that includes Work and Family Balance, Made By and For Moms, Baby Product Guide, Online Banking, Women-Owned Businesses, Online Job Search, Your Baby Today, Fun Family Activities, Beauty and Style Your Way, and a Tools and Checklists segment.

I've taken the "Who We Are" portion from the site (www.Bluesuitmom.com), and, as you can see, these are definitely women who have spent time juggling work and family separation:

Maria Bailey, CEO and Founder
    Ms. Bailey is the Founder and has served as President of BlueSuitMom.com, Inc since its inception in 1999. Ms. Bailey has over 20

years experience in business with a concentration in publishing, marketing and business development. Most recently she served as Vice President at AutoNation USA, formerly Republic Industries, where she reported directly to the Co-CEO during the years when Republic was named as America's #1 fastest growing company by Forbes magazine. She created and launched the first loyalty-marketing program within the automotive industry while at AutoNation.

Prior to AutoNation, Ms. Bailey ran Bailey Innovative Marketing, which served clients such as Discovery Zone, The Miami Herald and Broward Community College. Her involvement with Broward Community College included serving as interim Executive Director of the BCC Foundation managing assets of over $15 million. In 1990, she created and produced The South Florida Parenting Conference, which today is the largest parenting conference in Florida. She began her career with McDonald's Restaurants and The Miami Herald where she held a variety of management positions. She is the author of *The Women's Home-Based Business Book of Answers*. Ms. Bailey is published in Child Magazine, South Florida Parenting Magazine, The Miami Herald, and Family Times Magazine. She is the mother of four children, wife to Tim Bailey and a marathon runner.

Rachael P. Bender, Co-Founder and Vice President of Technology and Content

Ms. Bender brings Internet and Web design experience from many popular sites. Prior to BlueSuitMom.com, Ms. Bender worked at various parenting Web sites. Her contributions at Cox Interactive Media included web production on GoPBI.com, SoFla.com, Lightning Stalker.com and Sunfest.org. Ms. Bender not only brings strong technology experience to BlueSuitMom.com but a background in journalism as well. She spent several years working with and is published in Florida Today.

Paula Levenson, Director of Communications

Ms. Levenson brings a strong background in marketing and communications to her position at BlueSuitMom.com. She has been a business consultant to many of South Florida's largest companies. This, along with a postgraduate degree in elementary education from McGill University in her native Montreal, provides her with a unique perspective of childhood growth and development. Ms. Levenson was the Director of Programming for Another Generation Preschools, one of the nation's largest preschool chains, prior to its acquisition by Nobel Education. She is the mother of four children.

Marti Zenor, Director of Marketing Communications

Ms. Zenor contributes over 20 years of consumer marketing, public relations, marketing communications and business development to BlueSuitMom.com. Most recently she served as the Manager of New Media Communications for AutoNation USA, the largest automobile retailer in the USA and parent company to Alamo Rent A Car and National Car Rental. Prior to AutoNation, Ms. Zenor managed national promotions and merchandising for Discovery Zone, the children's entertainment company. Prior to joining Discovery Zone, Ms. Zenor was owner and founder of Grafik Language, a graphic design firm in San Diego. Ms. Zenor has also held marketing management positions for Mail Boxes Etc. and several women-owned businesses. She is the mother of one.

Jorj Morgan, Lifestyle Editor

Ms. Morgan's expertise in the culinary field incorporates 25 years of entertaining as well as owning a successful catering company. She is the author of *At Home In The Kitchen* and the mother of three boys.

Bluesuitmom also has an impressive list of regular experts and contributors that includes attorneys, business advisors/coaches, clinical social workers, early childhood specialists, parent educators, and pediatricians.

IVILLAGE: THE NETWORK FOR WOMEN

This may be one of the best-known sites devoted to women. They have been online since 1995 and carry a wide variety of news and information that includes segments on parenting from toddlers to teens and on working mothers. You can join in, or establish, chat rooms where you can explore topics that you may want to discuss with other women. Ivillage is not focused on the working mother per se, but they fully embrace the choices women face today. They have more than 3,000 different message boards as well as many ideas for stay-at-home moms, working moms, traveling moms, and moms with home businesses.

For more information check their website at www.ivillage.com

WYNDHAM HOTELS
AND WOMEN ON THE WAY

Many of the large hotel and resort corporations have specialized travel programs. The rise in women business travelers has been noted, and Wyndham is one that took the concept into a complete program. The focus is not exclusive to traveling with children, but the surveys they conduct and the Women on the Way newsletter provides useful information about any topic women choose to discuss. The following is from the www.wyndham.com site:

> Created in 1995, the Women On Their Way program has allowed Wyndham to develop an ongoing dialogue with a core group of customers—women business travelers. Through an annual contest and survey, the chain's dedicated Website feature, and the involvement of Wyndham's Advisory Board of Women Business Travelers, the company has been able to both solicit and respond to feedback regarding its amenities and services.
>
> "We value the opinions of women business travelers who have the expertise necessary to make acute assessments of our room service program," said Cary Broussard, Vice President of Women On Their Way Marketing. "Their feedback helps us to improve the experience not just for other women business travelers, but for all of our customers."

This, then, is the end of Part Two, even though there are, no doubt, a number of sites and support organizations that have been established since I sent the manuscript to the publisher. I know that many families are already involved with community, neighborhood, or religious-affiliated groups, and I haven't really discussed those in this section. Some families have no need or desire to join structured organizations, but the information provided in the preceding pages can be a good place to start for those who may be in search of external interaction.

Notes

CHAPTER ONE

1. Jane Seaberry, "Business Travel Continues to Increase," *Dallas Morning News*, December 5, 1999.
2. John Gray, *Children Are From Heaven* (New York: Harper Collins Book, 1999), pp. 22-23.
3. "Active Duty Military Personnel Strengths by Regional Area and By Country," (Department of Defense, Directorate for Information Operations and Reports, as of September 30, 2001).

CHAPTER THREE

1. Terri Apter, *The Confident Child* (New York: W.W. Norton & Co, 1997), pp. 52-53.
2. Stanley Turecki, with Sarah Wernick, *The Emotional Problems of Normal Children* (New York: Bantam Books, 1994), p. 203.

CHAPTER FOUR

1. Lawrence Kutner, *Making Sense of Your Teenager* (New York: William Morrow and Co., 1997), p. 27.
2. Laura Stepp Sessions, *Our Last Best Shot: Guiding Our Children Through Early Adolescence* (New York: Riverhead Books, 2000), p. 3.
3. Joseph P. Shapiro, "Teenage Wasteland?" *U.S. News & World Report*, October 23, 1995, p. 84.

4. James C. Dobson, *Parenting Isn't for Cowards* (Waco, Tex.: World Books, 1987), pp.151-152.
5. Peter Jensen, "Home, But Not Alone," *Baltimore Sun*, March 5, 2000, p. 4N.

CHAPTER SIX

1. Irwin Matus, *Wrestling With Parenthood* (Littleton, Colo.: Gylantic Publishing, 1995), p. 24.
2. Ellen Galinsky, *Ask The Children: What America's Children Really Think About Working Parents* (New York: William Morrow and Co., 1999), pp. 16-17.
3. Ibid., pp. 331-355.
4. Cindy Loose, "The Guilt, The Guilt," *Washington Post*, May 20, 2001, p. E10.
5. Matus, pp. 108-109.
6. Herman Roiphe and Anne Roiphe, *The Complete Guide to Infant and Child Emotional Well-Being* (New York: St. Martin's Press, 1985), p. 53

CHAPTER NINE

1. Lawrence Kutner, *Making Sense of Your Teenager* (New York: William Morrow and Co., 1997), p. 203.

PART TWO

1. Kathleen Welker, "Commentary: Army Celebrates 25th Anniversary of All-Volunteer Force," Army News Service, July 13, 1998 (Washington).
2. Edna J. Hunter, Ed., "Changing Families in a Changing Military System," (Symposium Proceedings, Military Family Research Conference, Naval Health Research Center, San Diego, Calif., 1977), pp. v-vi.
3. G. W. Yeatman, "Paternal Separation and the Military Dependent Child," *Military Medicine*, Vol. 146, May 1981, p. 320.
4. Ibid., p. 322.
5. Wayne Blount, Amos Curry, and Gerald I. Lubin, "Family Separations in the Military," *Military Medicine*, Vol. 157, February 1992, p. 76

6. Morton G. Ender, "E-mail to Somalia: New Communication Media Between Home and War-Fronts," Technical Report in Behar, J.E., *Mapping Cyberspace: Social Research on the Electronic Frontier,* Dowling College Press, Long Island, N.Y.), 1997 p. 31.

7. Ibid., pp. 38-42.

8. Navy Leadership Study (Military Family Resource Center, Arlington, Va., 1999), chart 93.

9. U.S. Department of Defense News Release 153-02, The Pentagon, March 27, 2002.

10. Suzanne Braun Levine, "The Good Daddy," *Ladies Home Journal,* April 2000.

11. "Family Structure and Children's Living Arrangments," *America's Childen: Key National Indicators of Well-Being,* pp. 6-7. Report issued by the Federal Interagency Forum on Child and Family Statistics, July 2001. Available from *www.ChildStats.gov.*

Select Bibliography

Amen, D.G., I. Jellen, E. Merves, and R. E. Lee. "Minimizing the Impact of Deployment Separation on Military Children; Stages, Current Preventive Efforts and System Recommendations." (1988).

Apter, Terri. *The Confident Child.* New York: W.W. Norton & Co., 1997.

Arp, David H., Claudia S. Arp, Scott M. Stanley, Howard J. Markman, and Susan L. Blumberg. *Fighting for Your Empty Nest Marriage.* San Francisco: Jossey-Bass, 2000.

Blount, Wayne, Amos Curry, and Gerald I. Lubin. "Family Separations in the Military." *Military Medicine,* Vol. 157, February 1992, pp. 76-80.

Boothby, Rita. *The Golden Rules of Parenting.* Sterling, Va.: Capital Books, 2001.

Brown, Ruth Meyer. *A Grandmother's Guide To Extended Babysitting,* Sterling, Va.: Capital Books, 2001.

Brownlee, Shannon, and Matthew Miller. "5 Lies Parents Tell Themselves About Why They Work." *U.S. News and World Report,* (May 12, 1997).

Dickerson, W., and R. Arthur. "Navy Families in Distress." (1965).

Dobson, James C. *Parenting Isn't for Cowards.* Waco, Tex.: World Books, 1987.

Ender, M.G. "E-mail to Somalia: New Communication Media Between Home and War-Fronts." (1997).

Felice, Marianne, and Susan Satow. "Growing Up Without Tears." *Good Housekeeping* (September 1993).

Galinsky Ellen. *Ask The Children: What America's Children Really Think About Working Parents.* New York: William Morrow and Co., 1999.

Gray, John. *Children Are From Heaven.* New York: Harper Collins Books, 1999.

Herbst, Ann Colin. "10 Surprising Reasons Your Kids Act Up." *Redbook* (August 1997).

Hill, Ruth. "More Business Travelers Are Taking Kids Along." *Denver Business Journal* (May 5, 2000).

Holman, Jennifer Reid. "Home or Away: The Dilemma of Motherhood." *Better Homes and Gardens* (October 1999).

Hunt, Mary. *Debt Proof Your Kids.* Nashville, Tenn.: Broadman & Holman Publishers, 1998.

Hunter, E.J., ed. "Changing Families in a Changing Military System." *Military Family Research Conference* Naval Health Research Center, San Diego, Calif. (1977).

Jensen, Peter. "Home, But Not Alone." *Baltimore Sun* (March 5, 2000).

Kane, Frank L., and Leigh Anne Nicholson Bathke. "Your Child's Development: Birth to Preschool." *Newsweek* (September 29, 1997).

Kutner, Lawrence. *Making Sense of Your Teenager.* New York: William Morrow and Co., 1997.

Labich, Kenneth. "Can Your Career Hurt Your Kids?" *Fortune* (May 20, 1991).

Lansky, Vicki. *Trouble Free Travel with Children: Helpful Hints for Parents on the Go.* Minnetonka, Minn.: Book Peddlers, 1996.

Levine, Suzanne Braun. "The Good Daddy." *Ladies Home Journal* (April 2000).

Loose, Cindy. "The Guilt, The Guilt." *Washington Post* (May 20, 2001).

Matus, Irwin. *Wrestling With Parenthood.* Littleton, Colo.: Gylantic Publishing, 1995.

McNair, James. "Extended Stay America Finds Niche in Value-Seeking Travelers." *Knight-Ridder/Tribune Business News* (February 7, 2000).

Noonan, Peggy. "Looking Forward: What Really Makes Kids Happy." *Good Housekeeping* (January 1998).

Phelen, Thomas W. *Surviving Your Adolescents*. 2nd ed., Child Management, Inc., Glen Ellyn, Ill. 1998.

Raskin, Robin. "Parents Who Travel and the Kids Who Need Them." *FamilyPC* (May 2000).

Roiphe, Herman and Anne Roiphe. *Your Child's Mind: The Complete Guide to Infant and Child Emotional Well-Being*, New York: St. Martin's Press, 1985.

Rosebaum, M. "Emotional Aspects of Wartime Separations." *The Family Journal* (1944).

Schroeder, Deborah and Judith Waldrop. "How Business Travelers Are Changing." *American Demographics* (November 1992).

Seaberry, Jane. "Business Travel Continues to Increase." *Dallas Morning News* (December 5, 1999)

Sessions, Laura Stepp. *Our Last Best Shot: Guiding Our Children Through Early Adolescence*. New York: Riverhead Books, 2000.

Shapiro, Joseph P. "Teenage Wasteland? (Early Adolescence)." *U.S. News & World Report* (October 23, 1995).

Tristam, Claire with Lucille Tristram. *Have Kids Will Travel: 101 Survival Strategies for Vacationing with Babies and Young Children*. Kansas City, Mo.: Andrews McMeel Publishing, 1997.

Turecki, Stanley and Sarah Wernick. *The Emotional Problems of Normal Children*, New York: Bantam Books, 1994.

Yeatman, G.W. "Paternal Separation and the Military Dependent Child." *Military Medicine* (May 1981).

Index

adult offspring, return of, 75–79
AFLO. See Army Family Liaison Office
AFTB. See Army Family Team Building
age groups
    years 0–2, 10–14
    years 3–5, 14–18
    years 6–10, 21–24
    years 11–12, 24–26
    years 13–14, 35–36
    years 15–18, 37–38
Air Force, family resources, 121–24
Allen, Ed, 64
Apter, Terri, 23
Army Family Liaison Office (AFLO), 124
Army Family Team Building (AFTB), 125–26
audio books, 67–68

babies, 10–14
Bailey, Maria, 7, 30, 136–37
balance
    importance of, 96–97
    lack of, 92–93

for single parents, 86–87
in time with/away from family, 49–53
Bender, Rachel, 136–37
Bernard, Jacqueline, 134–35
blood type, 46–47
Blount, Wayne, 115–16
Bluesuitmom, 7, 30, 136–38
Broussard, Cary, 139

cameras
    digital, 62–63
    for missed events, 12
    video, 22, 62–63
canceling travel, for illness, 47
caretakers
    during family travel, 29–30
    of infants, 12
    single parents and, 28–29
checklists, 98–107
collections, on destinations, 22
communicating, 94–97
    e-mail, 23–24
    about illness, 47
    with preschoolers, 15–17

communicating (*continued*)
  with preteens, 25
  about purpose of travel, 85–86
  about school, 22–23
  technology for, 57–64
  with teens, 38, 41–42
computers, 60
  for young children, 64
Curry, Amos, 115–16

dental emergencies, 46
Department of Defense (DOD)
  homepage, 120
  resources for families, 111–29
digital cameras, 62–63
Dobson, James, 37
DOD. See Department of Defense
DVD players, portable, 67

Egleson, Jim, 134
elementary schoolers, 21–24
Elliott, Brenda, 83
e-mail, 23–24, 61–62
  features of, 62–63
emergencies
  dealing with, 43–47
  planning for, 45–47, 98–99
emotions
  mixed, 87–88
  valuing, 54–56
empty-nest issues, 73–79
  Empty Nest As a Place to Visit
    checklist, 107
Ender, Morton G., 117
Enyart, Marcia, 81
extended family, 17
  living arrangements of, 78–79
  stories of, 91–92

facsimile (fax) machines, 60
family constitution, 31–33
family dinner, on return, 28

Family Readiness Groups (FRGs),
  125
family travel, 29–31
firsts, missing, dealing with, 11–12
flying
  with children, 68–69
  children alone, 69–72, 103
Flying a Minor Unaccompanied
  checklist, 103
FRGs. See Family Readiness Groups

Galinsky, Ellen, 49–50
game systems, 67–68
Get-Around-To-It list, 99
Gissiner, Carrie, 83, 129
good-byes, with preschoolers, 18
grandparents, stories of, 91–92
Gray, John, 5
guilt
  respecting, 54–56
  teens on, 52–53
  about travel, 49

Hall, G. Stanley, 36
home alone, 38–40
  checklist for, 106
Hunt, Mary, 78
Hunter, Edna J., 113

infants, 10–14
instant messaging, 62
Internet, 23–24, 61–62
  features of, 62–63
Internet service providers (ISPs), 61
iVillage, 138

Jensen, Peter, 38

Kutner, Lawrence, 35, 75

laptops, 67
Larson, Aaron, 132
Ledbetter, Eileen, 82

Levenson, Paula, 137–38
Levine, Susanne Braun, 131–32
Loose, Cindy, 51
Lubin, Gerald I., 115–16

Marine Corps, family resources, 126
Matus, Irwin, 49, 51
Medical and Emergency Treatment checklist, 46, 98
medical emergencies, dealing with, 43–47
men
    as at-home parents, 88–90
    as frequent travelers, 90–91, 93
    resources for, 131–34
MFRC. See Military Family Resource Center
military
    resources for families, 111–29
    stories of, 81–86
    and travel, 6–7, 48–49
Military Brat Network, 129
Military Family Resource Center (MFRC), 120–21
Military Teens on the Move (MTOM), 121
missing important events, dealing with, 11–12, 22
Morgan, Jorj, 138
Mother's Aides, 30
MP3 players, 63
MTOM. See Military Teens on the Move
music, 67–68

National Guard, family resources, 126–29
National Long Distance Relationship Building Institute, 132–34
Navy, family resources, 126

overnight alone, 38–40
    checklist for, 106

pagers, 58–60
parents
    and empty nest, 73–74, 79
    and issue of travel, 48–56, 92–93
    reactions to travel, 10–11, 25–26
Parents Without Partners (PWP), 134–36
preschoolers, 14–18
    computers and, 64
presents
    for preschoolers, 18–19
    and resentment, 13
    wish lists for, 100–102
preteens, 24–26
project planning checklist, 99
PWP. See Parents Without Partners

quality of life issues (QOL), in military families, 112

resentment
    on return, 13, 52
    stories of, 87–88
Reserve, family resources, 126–29
restricting travel, 53–54
    with teens, 38
returns
    with infants, 13, 52
    with preteens, 27–28
Roiphes, Anne and Herman, 52
routines, adjusting, 58
    with babies, 12
    with preteens, 26–27

school, communicating about, 22–23
security measures, at airports, 69
separation
    dealing with, 52
    emotional reactions to, 54–56, 92–93
    empty nest and, 73–74, 79
    in military families, 114–15, 123–24

separation *(continued)*
  realities of, 3–5
separation anxiety, 5–6
  and illness, 47
  in preteens, 25
September 11, 2001
  and airport security, 69
  and worries about travel, 23
Sergeant Mom's, 129–31
Shapiro, Joseph P., 35–36
Should I Take the Family Along?
  checklist, 104–5
single parents, 28–29
  resources for, 134–36
  and responsibilities of children,
    40–41
  stories of, 86–87
Stepp, Laura Sessions, 35
stress-related illnesses, 47
Sugarman, Joan G., 31–33
support people, 17

technology, 57–65
  cameras, 12, 22, 62–63
  computers, 60, 64
  difficulties with, 64–65
  e-mail, 23–24, 61–63
  and military families, 117–18
teens, 34–42
  limits of, 40–42
  on parent travel, 52–53
  preparing for leaving home,
    77–79, 107
telephone, 58–60
text messaging, 59
time intervals, defining for child,
  14–16
toddlers, 10–14
travel
  checklists on, 98–107

children alone, 69–72, 103
  debate on, 48–56
  with family, 29–31, 104–5
  frequent, 90–91
  purpose of, 85–86
  restricting, 38, 53–54
  safety of, worries about, 23
  unexpected, 83–86
Truesdale, Janet, 81
Turecki, Stanley, 25

vehicle television-video systems, 67
video camera, 62–63
  for missed events, 22
video conferencing, 62

warning signs
  in infants, 13
  of too much travel, 53–54
web cameras, 62
week, defining for child, 14–16
Wernick, Sarah, 25
What Did You Bring Me? list, 100–102
When to Leave a Teen Alone
  Overnight checklist, 106
women
  as at-home parent, 82–83
  resources for, 136–39
  travelers, 81
Women on the Way, 139
worries
  addressing, 16–18
  dealing with, 43–47
  about safety of travel, 23
Wyndham Hotels, women's
  resources, 139

Yeatman, Gentry W., 114–15

Zenor, Marti, 138